REVELATIONS

of

LITTLE JOHN

My journey,

From the Horns to the Cross

True Story:

Written and Designed By: John R. Burnett Jr.
Edited By: Brandy Wadsworth
Inspired By: The Holy Spirit

Dedicated **t**o:

GOD, The Holy Spirit,

G.J.B,

&

The

souls lost in the dark

"My son, do not forget my teachings. Keep my commands in your heart. They will help you live for many years. They will bring you success. Don't let love and truth ever leave you. Tie them around your neck. Write them on the tablet of your heart."- Proverbs 3: 1-3

Δ-Δ-Δ Revelations Δf Little John Δ-Δ-Δ

Printed and distributed by: Book Baby Publishing
BookBaby.com
First printed: March 2022

John R. Burnett Jr.

revelationsoflittlejohn@gmail.com

P.O. Box 702060

Saint, Cloud, FL, 34770

.

T.O.C.

Δ-Δ-Δ Revelations Δf Little John Δ-Δ-Δ

"But the Farther will send the Friend in my name to help you, The Friend is the Holy Spirit. He will teach you all things."- John14:26 (full verse in appendix.)

❤ PREFACE ❤

Throughout life I have experienced my fair share of traumas. I learned at a young age to hold in the pain, until eventually it would come out in the most horrific ways. Then I would always have to pay the consequences for my actions. People close to me, including my psychiatrist, have told me I should journal or talk to someone about what troubles me in life. Most of them have not lived a life like mine to understand me. So, I have never understood why I should discuss what bothers me to anyone.

However, a person can only hold so much pain and anger in. Before they start hating themselves and others. Then everything you're holding in, will come out in some way, good or bad. Recently finding a deeper love for God and myself, has help me realize that holding in my pain or trying to mask it in any way only made things worse for me overall. Because I know what happens when I let the pain out in the bad ways. Journaling has been weighing heavy on my heart and mind.

This book is not to hurt, slander, or put blame on anybody involved in it. It's only me journaling to share the challenging times I have faced through my own life. How not dealing with my problems or trying to hide the pain only caused me further damage. For that reason, I have changed a few characters' names throughout the story for their own privacy. A little forewarning this story goes deep and dark in my life. However, what is done in the dark will always be brought to the light.

The Holy Spirit inspired me to author this journal in case something happens to me, and my son finds himself lost in life. For him to understand its ok to seek help for whatever troubles him mentally or physically, over choosing self-destruction. Secondly, to help as many people as I can change their outlook on life for the better of all. I have personally learned this life is what each person chooses to make out of it. Every action I have ever taken had a reaction, and every choice I have ever made had a consequence, good or bad.

Heather and Little John

"Then does it not guide them when they see how many generations We destroyed before them as they walk among their dwellings? Indeed, there are signs in that for those of intelligence."-

Quran 20:128

Location in appendix

♥ Hello Friends ♥

We could start with me in the beginning. However, the traumas and drama start in the family generations before that. Nonetheless when I, Little John, was born into this world on 9/14/1989. My parents were facing their own untreated problems. Mom's name is Stephanie Marie Ray. She is from Alabama, and has two sisters, Mendy, and Cynthia.

Moms' family moved to Florida, when the girls were younger. She was born to a, Edgar, and Glenda Marie Ray (Granny). Grand dad was a disabled Air Force veteran. Who had lymphoma cancer and eventually passed away.

Granny always said he was an amazing man. Sadly, this happen when mom was around eight years old. Edgar's death was devastating to the family and extremely hard on my mom. It's said she was a daddy's girl growing up.

Now granny found herself raising two little girls alone. Later, giving birth to my Aunt Cynthia. Throughout life granny has always been a caring, loving parent and grandmother. Not to mention, has always gone beyond for everyone in our family. Over the years it is said, mom became an uncontrollable teen. She started partying and running away from home. Then eventually found herself drinking and using drugs. I'm guessing to hide her pain. Even though mom had a rough life, I have to say she has always had a big heart and loved us in her own unique way.

Along the timeline, she met John R. Burnett Sr., through friends and family. My dad, Big John, also moved to Florida when he was younger. With his parents, Papa James and Grandma Irene Burnett. Not to mention, dad has five siblings, Juanita, Donna, Rick, Ronnie, and Debbie. Thier family is from the Michigan, Ohio, area

Northern United Sates. Throughout life Big John has always had a big heart but could be very scary when he gets angry. Dad is over six feet tall, and his arms look like most people's thighs.

When Sr. was growing up, Papa James was the nicest guy. On the other hand, he wasn't so lovely when he would start drinking as stories were told. Then he became abusive and a terrifying person. From some of the story's I've heard he would beat my grandma and the kids when dad was younger. Grandma Irene was always a loving, caring, straight forward woman. Not to mention, the best cook I knew.

There is no doubt my parents both faced troubled life's before I was born, and that's their own stories to share. However, the ways they coped with their problems only hurt them and us kids. Which leads to my story. People may tell you I'm an insane, delusional, jackass. Some will even say, I am the devil. I hope the ones who truly know me will say I was a God loving, funny, free spirit, Ace of Jack's with the biggest heart. I always found joy in making other people laugh and smile. However, when the pain I was holding in became too much for me. I would always show out in the worst ways.

If you can keep a secret! I will share a few untold details of my life with you. I will start from birth and adventure through life into the present. Bear with me, my speech impediment and brain injury as I try to journal back in time. Sharing my personal traumas, violence, drug problems, and the heartaches I have faced. I'm Praying, we all can have a better understanding life doesn't always go as we plan, and terrible things happen to everyone. To know if you're struggling in life physically or mentally, to go seek help over choosing to hide your pain or following a path of self-destruction.

Every person is different, but we are all holding in pain, secrets, and traumas in some form that's causing us to suffer. We all face horrible things that nobody wants to talk about to others. The sad part is the more pain a person holds in. Eventually, it turns to hate and tends to hurt them, and the people close to them the most. Not to mention, how toxic things can keep you from living a long, peaceful, prosperous life.

Friends, it's always better to ask for help or forgiveness. Rather than choosing to hold in so much negativity or trying to mask your pain in any way. However, that may be, seeking God, talking to a doctor, being around friends and family, meditating, or even writing. Regardless how you might choose to get rid of the negativity in your life. Releasing the bad without hurting yourself or someone else is always better than letting it turn into hate believe me. I know it is easier to say these things than to do them. For that reason, here are some of my darkest secrets. First make sure your heart is open, hold on tight to your faith and religion. This here is my story!

"Even though I walk through the darkest valley, I will not be afraid. You are with me. Your shepherd's rod and staff comfort me."- Psalms 23:4

❤ Childhood Nightmares ❤

So it begins, sometime in the 80s and along the way, my mom and dad met in Saint Cloud, Florida. Quickly they fell in love, and life began good for them. From the tales I've heard over the years, there was a lot of being around friends and family, drinking, using drugs, and mud bogging during these times.

My mom cleaned houses, and dad is by far the best mechanic I know. They ended up getting married and having my sister Heather. She is three years older than me and knows more about these times. Over the years, my parents drinking, and drug usage grew even more out of control. Mom has told me before, that she was pregnant with me for months and didn't even know.

I'm not saying they weren't good times as a toddler. I'm sure there were a ton of great moments. My parents have told me stories of when I was a baby and how I was a wild child. When I was a couple of years old my Papa James passed away. Momma said something mentally changed in my dad during these times. From here, I'm guessing the alcohol, drugs, and fighting got even worse for both.

The sad part is that some of my earliest childhood memories were of my mom and dad fighting. I can't tell you what the fights were over. All I can say is seeing my dad hit my mom and vice versus was terrifying. The screaming and hitting would haunt me at night. Mom ended up leaving when I was around five and I don't know all the details why, again that's their story. However, Heather and my lives would change forever. (Story continues after picture).

Heather and Little John.

During these times I developed horrific nightmares. These weren't regular nightmares. I would scream bloody murder in my sleep. As a kid, sleeping over at someone's house was always embarrassing. Every time no matter where I was or who I was with, I would have these nightmares. Not to mention how terrifying it had to be on whomever I may have stayed with at the time. The way I would scream in my sleep was said to be like someone was trying to kill me.

After mom left, dad quit using drugs and started working hard on being a good parent to us. He was able to get us a trailer in a mobile home park. Showed us nothing but love, and overall life was starting to get better for us. Dad and mom even tried to work things out for a bit. I'm guessing it was for me and my sister's sake. Sometime after mom left again, sadly dad started going downhill.

Around six years old, we started living with my grandma Irene who lived in Narcoossee, Florida. These were fun times for me because Aunt Debbie and our cousin TJ also lived there. TJ is between mine and

Heather's age. Plus, the street that grandma lived on had kids at every house, and it was found on East Lake Tohopekaliga. The one on the front book cover to be exact.

We had a private boat ramp and the most significant lakefront property on the road. Us kids grew up fishing, building clubhouses, swimming in the lake, and was always exploring nature. TJ and I were getting our butts whooped daily. You can say we were very adventurous, wild kids.

Over time my dad would run into Pamela Caves she has five children herself. Dad and Pam had known each other for years. In saying that Pam had always been around Heather and me while our mom and dad were together. However now both being single they started dating. At first dad, Heather, and I still lived with Grandma Irene. Pam and her kids lived on their own and would come visit us on the weekends. I always felt like more kids to play with meant more fun. Not to mention we all had a lot of daring adventures together and have all grown close over the years.

One day TJ and I were trying to catch a small alligator at our boat ramp. It took us a week before we finally captured it. I lured it up the boat ramp with the raw chicken. TJ was able to get it hooked and tied. Off to the house, we went dragging the gator. We got Big John to come outside. Wanting to show him what we had caught. Dad cut that gator loose, laughed, and swatted it back to the lake. TJ and I were furious like no other. We wanted him to cook it.

Nonetheless the next time TJ and I were fishing probably up to no good. When we caught a big alligator gar. Quickly, it was decided not to tell anyone about the fish, and we decided to throw the gar in a porta-john up the street. This company was building a housing development on our road and as kids thought it would be funny. We did just that, walked up there, and threw it in the Honey bucket.

Everyday walking home from the school bus, we would stop and kick that porta-loo. That fish would then go nuts inside there. It would start splashing and rocking that Jonny-on-the-spot all over. I could only imagine a worker's face when they used the bathroom, and that fish went to splashing. That thing was in there for weeks someone had to sit on that Spiffy Biff at least one time. (Story continues after picture).

Little John fishing @ Moss Park, Fl.

Pam was always friendly to Heather and me in the beginning. She worked at the local gas station and would give us free stuff when we went there. In no time, we were all living together. We would stay with grandma, then later started moving around a lot. Somewhere along the lines, it became a nightmare. Heather and I started losing our dad's focus. Pam and dad started doing drugs and fighting all the time. Not just arguing actual fist fighting too.

As a kid while living at Grandmas house, all the adults staying there were on drugs except Grandma. They would fistfight and holler when they didn't have drugs or money. I can remember one morning all of us kids, sitting at the table, eating. When Big John and Aunt Debbie started beating the mess out of each other. All over the kitchen, for whatever reason. It seemed to happen all the time and wasn't unusual for someone to always be fighting.

When I was around seven, close to eight, we now found ourselves living around Pam's family. Again, we were always back and forth. Her parents owned and worked a lawn business. Plus, they had other business adventures with the rest of Pam's family. As a kid, during the summer, we would all go to work for her parents. Either mowing yards, cleaning houses, or selling corn, sometimes all three. These was fun times unbelievably.

Pam's parents didn't do drugs or fight at their house, and it wasn't aloud there. Plus, we were able to keep the stuff left behind, when we cleaned the houses. It was like a big treasure hunt as a kid. My dad and Pam eventually rented the trailer a couple of doors down from her parent's house. This neighborhood was surrounded by mother nature for miles. After school, we would build tree houses, play hide-and-seek, and explore woods for hours. Sometime while living on our own again dad and Pam were back to using drugs heavy.

During these times, my stepbrother and I would go stay nights at Bob's house with his kids. Bob is like a brother to Pam and my dad. Our sisters would go to Pam's sisters' house to stay for the weekend. It started as a nice little break compared to what we went through. Uncle Bob had the best snacks, and his kids had the best toys. It was so enjoyable over there.

Until one day, Bob's stepson started messing with me sexually. As a little kid, I thought this was ok. Plus, I always heard the adults talking about sexual things. So, it made me think it was normal. However, something inside me knew it wasn't right and it would make me feel bad about myself. During these times I always felt like I didn't have anyone to talk to about my feelings. So, I just held those feelings in.

As time went on things kept getting worse. I remember me and my stepsister started sneaking in our parents' room when they weren't home and looking at their porn magazines. We wouldn't do anything together. She would read them, and I would just look at the boobs as I couldn't fully read yet. Eventually, I started doing these things I was seeing in these magazines with other kids I was around.

I cannot remember exactly if we got caught doing something bad or someone told on us. All I can say is that people close to my stepmom made me feel disgusting and horrible. I understand their reasoning now, but I didn't understand as a kid. The funny thing is that no one ever wanted to know why I was doing these things or where I had learned them.

Around these times my dad had went to jail which wasn't unusual. The police were always after him for something. This one time, they came in our house looking for him, and he managed to hide in the dirty clothes pile. One police officer even kicked the pile of clothes he was under. Standing there watching this I could not believe they didn't find him that night.

Nonetheless, dad was now locked up, and Pam's parents was still buying the trailers full of corn. The family would take turns sitting on the side of the road, selling it to the passing cars. One day I was running from the corn trailer to the house, and the grass was high. Not to mention I didn't have any shoes on.

When suddenly, I stepped on a pitchfork sticking up in the grass. The sharpest points went right through my foot. Through the bottom and out of the top! At first, I didn't know what happened. I just hit the ground as I was running along, and then noticed my foot was hard to move. That's when I saw the pitchfork through my foot. Then I had to pull it out of my foot to be able to move.

By now Pam had come running outside and rushed me to the hospital. Not to mention she even took great care of me during recovery. The doctors said I was lucky, because if I had pulled it out the wrong way. I possibly could have caused severe damage. I ended up with stitches and had to use crutches for a brief time.

So be it, as a family we faced a lot of hard times. It seemed like every time the rent was due, we found ourselves moving more and more. Not just from the drugs but having six children had to be tough on dad and Pam financially as well. As a family we knew what broke was but somehow always managed to make it by.

One time that always stood out to me the most. We were living in a mobile home park, and money was tight. We weren't going to celebrate Christmas at home that year, and us kids knew it. All our spirits were broken or down, you could say. When this man showed up at the house one day close to Christmas.

He had a truckload of beautifully wrapped presents! There weren't any names on them, and they were all elegantly dressed in the same paper. The man seemed to know which gifts was for each of us without hesitation. It was the most magical moment I had experienced as a kid.

He was not dressed as the Santa we see on television, just in regular clothes. He didn't stop at any other houses after giving us the presents. Big John and Pam didn't know him. We had never seen him before or after that day. It really was a special moment in my life. Around this time, the violence and drugs became unbearable again. Heather was becoming our mom in a way. She would cook, clean, get us kids up and ready for school. Her nickname was even Cinderella.

During these years, granny and Aunt Cynthia would come pick up, Heather and me for a weekend every month. Oh, how we love these trips as kids. They showed Heather and me, unconditional love like no other. We would always go to McDonald's for chicken nugget happy meals. Then off to Lake Helen, where granny lived. These weekends really were peaceful and joyful to us.

Lake Helen really was Heaven on Earth to us as kids. We could ride our bikes anywhere in the town. Granny's sister, Aunt Pat and her husband Uncle Pete lived on the next street as granny. Every time we visited them, Uncle

Pete would give us each five dollars and always take us to Taco Bell. After, Heather and I would always go to the store up the street for candy. Then to the library to check out VHS tapes for the weekend. Not to mention granny showed us nothing but love the whole time. (Story continues after picture).

Irene, Heather, Stephanie, Little John

This one week in particular, mom was going to be at granny's house. It had been a while since we had seen her, and still had a couple of days before they were supposed to pick us up. However, Pam was making this stuff she calls Pammy surprise for dinner one night. It is a soup with everything in it. It personally reminds me of pig slop. My dad, on the other hand, loves the stuff. Knowing my mother was coming around, you could say I had a whole different attitude.

I informed Pam I was a king, and they didn't eat that. We argued, then she ended up backhanding me in my mouth and busting my lip. I would tell you she almost took my dang lip off as a kid! Honestly, I could say it was just a minor scrape and swollen lip as an adult. However, this was our ticket away from there.

The weekend came, and it was time for us to go visit. This time however, Pam and dad had to send my stepsister with us, or we weren't allowed to go. We all three loaded up with granny and mom. Then we were on our way to granny's house. While driving down the road, mom noticed my lip right away. She lost her mind when I told her what had happened.

Once we got to granny's she called the police. Then informed them the situation and how she was taking Heather and myself from our dad. The next evening mom, Heather, and I boarded a Greyhound bus headed to Atlanta, Georgia, to live with mom and her boyfriend. Once granny knew we were out of state, she took my stepsister back to Big Johns. As my granny tells the story, she didn't stick around for my dad to come out. Granny will tell you she was scared for her life that day.

The bus ride to Atlanta wasn't that long. However, it was the first time I had ever been on a greyhound bus, making it all more exciting. Once the bus arrived, we moved in with mom's boyfriend Denny and his parents until our house was ready. These were new times and fun adventures for us. Mom was working hard to give us a good life. She even got us to start attending church and it was just what we needed. Denny and his dad had a garbage company. I was able to work with them during the off times from school.

Our house was eventually ready for us to move into. Now we were living in a mobile home park, and it was a blast. This park had a swimming pool. Somebody ran a candy store from one of the trailers and kids lived everywhere. I met friends and got to go to the Atlantic Braves baseball games. I even caught a foul ball in the stadium one time.

It wasn't long before Denny was on heroin, and my mom couldn't control Heather and myself. Mom and Heather were always bumping heads. Heather was now thirteen and grown. Mom never understood that Heather had already been treated like an adult and did the work of a grown woman. Now mom wanted to treat her like a kid again. I, myself, was super stubborn and didn't want to listen to anybody. It's safe to say it didn't work, and things got out of control quick. It seemed like everyone in the house was running wild.

So be it, mom wanted to go to Florida this one weekend to see her friends. Heather's guy friend had a car and was down for the adventure. After dropping our mom off in St. Augustine, Florida, none of us kids had any money. Quickly, the older guys we were with decide to rob a car wash for the change. Once successfully getting the money. We all met up with some stranger to get a bag of weed. This was the first time I had ever smoked

Marijuana in my life. I was so high and only nine years old at this point in life.

The weekend concluded and back to Georgia we went. Mom ended up going to jail when we got back home for whatever reason. So, Heather and I moved to Blackshear, Georgia. With Aunt Cynthia, our little cousin and her husband Bobby. Our aunt was very welcoming to Heather and me as she has always been. Bobby worked on an ostrich farm, and we could go to work with him when there wasn't school. Which was cool for me because I always got to drive the ATV's and do all kinds of fun things there.

As time went on, our aunt and Bobby started arguing a lot. I never knew why it was just getting to be more and more. Eventually, mom was released from jail in Atlanta and moved down to Blackshear with us. It wasn't long after we all started living together Aunt Cynthia moved back to Florida. I didn't know why she left at this point. I just knew they were gone.

Then it started, I came home from school one day after they moved out, and there was a brand-new stereo system at our house. This thing had speakers my size, all over the place. When Bobby turned the volume up on this radio, you could quickly hear it from half a mile away easy. For the next couple of months, Bobby and mom would throw big house parties. Drink, and do drugs what felt like non-stop.

One night during a party, I was woken by people arguing and fighting. When I opened the bedroom door, through all the commotion, I noticed this woman had her back toward me but was on top of my mom punching her. I was fed up with it all. I grabbed the closest thing to me, which happen to be a fishing pole. I kept swinging it as hard as I could every swing connected with this lady's back.

Every time I swung; all you could hear was the rod cutting through the air sounding like a whip as it connected. Every time it landed on her back; it would slice her skin straight open as she yelled in pain. I could see it was ripping through her skin because she was wearing a spaghetti strap shirt. All the adults had to hold me down and help her away about the fourth swing.

It wasn't long after that mom and Bobby decided to steal a bunch of old rare coins from their bosses at the farm. Then proceed to sell them at pawn shops all over North Florida and South Georgia. Once they offloaded all the coins, the police were on to them. I was woken up late one night when the police were at the house. Quickly, we had to make a run through the woods and swamp to Bobbys mom's house. Which was a good couple of miles away, and even further when you're a kid on a late-night adventure.

We soon decided to move to Jackson Hole, Wyoming, to evade police. By now, mom and Bobby knew they were wanted by the law and did not want to get arrested. Bobby, Heather, and I boarded a Greyhound bus bound for Wyoming. It took us five days, switching buses, traveling to different states, and meeting all kinds of people. What a journey it was! Mom was going to meet us in a couple of weeks. However, as she was getting ready to leave Georgia and boarded the Greyhound, the U.S. Marshalls arrested her.

Jackson Hole was a beautiful place; there was snow I had never seen. We made snowmen and snow angels.

There were new animals to me like elk, moose, chipmunks, and wild horses. Sometimes I would go to the candy stores and explore the town by myself. Bobby had bought me some ninjas throwing stars, and we would practice throwing them around town. Bobby, Heather, and I really bonded for that brief time.

One morning, I was getting ready for school. We were living in a hotel room, and I heard a knock at the door. Bobby informed me to hold on while he went to the bathroom. I didn't think much of it as I was still half asleep and had my shirt halfway over my head. As I pulled that shirt down and pulled on that door handle.

BOOM! That door flew open, and that foot that followed landed right in the center of my chest. As I flew across the room like a toy. "Don't fucking move!" was screamed, as people filled the room with vests, masks, and guns drawn. The Marshals took Bobby to jail and Heather and me to protective custody.

This turned out to be a good place for me. I learned to ski, understood how to be independent, and the counselors cared about us. More importantly, I finally found out why my aunt had left. Bobby had gotten my fourteen-year-old sister pregnant. After our mom was released from jail for the coin heist, she flew to Wyoming to bring Heather and myself back south. Heather moved back Blackshear to live with Bobbys parents. I would go to live with our granny in Lake Helen, Florida.

Around this time, I found myself in fifth grade and was riding my bike to school every day. As it wasn't too far from the house. Living with granny was awesome. She took good care of me and always showed me love. Plus, I didn't have to deal with what I was used to dealing with around her. As time progressed, I started hanging out with other troubled kids in the neighborhood; I picked up smoking cigarettes and weed more often. Found myself getting in trouble and not listening.

It is safe to say at some point granny could no longer control me, she always did her best with me, and tried to get me help. Granny would tell me about God and how good he was. I never wanted to listen. In my head, I always though what God would let this stuff happen to a kid. Eventually she decided I would go live with Tony and Matty in Blackshear, Georgia. Tony is Bobbys brother and has always been close friends to mom and our aunts. This would be the best thing for me at the time. I would have a positive manly figure in my life. Not to mention being able to be around Heather, my niece, and mom more.

"Faith is being sure of what we hope for. It is being certain of what we do not see."- Hebrews 11:1

♥ Confused Kid ♥

Fifth-grade graduation came, and shortly after it was time for me to move to Georgia with Tony and Matty. They welcomed me like one of their own children and always treated me as one. Tony and Matty have two kids: Caley and Neal around my age. This arrangement was fantastic because Heather and my newborn niece lived a couple of doors down from us.

Tony and Bobbys families always gathered for weekend dinners. They had a swimming pool and four wheelers. My mom was living right up the street with James, her boyfriend. Not to mention I was always back and forth between Tony and James.

When I first started staying around mom and James, we stayed with his parents. Him and his dad worked logging. So, when there wasn't school, I could ride in the semis with either of them. If we weren't hauling logs, we were in the woods preparing them for transporting. Staying with James was always a fun adventure; he wasn't on drugs and wasn't a violent person. To be honest one of best role models I had. Not to mention he took excellent care of mom and myself.

Back at Tony's, the adults partied a lot because their family all lived on the same property but different houses. On the weekends or after work, the family was always together. Most of them worked for Budweiser and would get all kinds of free things, banners, beers, and kegs. The parties would always be centered around the pool and end by the burn pit.

As a kid, it felt like the whole town would come to these parties. It was a sight to see! At the end of every party, there would be fistfights and drama. These events were before MMA was significant and was something to watch when you're young. Some of these fights were horrible, bloody, and gruesome. Not to mention my cousin TJ would come visit me during the summers. Which meant he could attend one of our biggest parties of the year.

Back at James house, all his family was big into NASCAR. Every weekend family and friends would gather over there to watch the races and cookout. We were always building different kinds of mud trucks or jeeps. Where he lives is surrounded by the swamp, so mudding was the life. His Aunt Linda and Uncle Lewis lived next door, and they always kept an eye on me when needed. You can say they kept me in line.

One time I was shooting James' nieces with the airsoft gun, and Aunt Linda got upset with me. She wanted to whoop my butt, so I run from her this time. I quickly decided; I would get naked and in the shower. In my mind, she couldn't whoop me in there. I promise when I tell you the door swung open. Then that shower curtain flew back, and she beat my wet ass like no other. Other than me being a wild child, things were going great. (Story continues after picture).

Heather, Stephanie, and Little John

Eventually, mom's drinking would start to get out of hand. This one incident I was in the sixth-seventh grade, and we were having a party at James house. Mom started getting really drunk and I could tell. When I tried to take the beer from mom and get her to go lay down. She got so mad at me. Then she was like you want it and threw the cup in the air. Resulting to the beer landing in my face. All I can say is my eyes were on fire.

Not to long after, mom and I were down the street from James at her friend's house. Somebody showed up with a bunch of cocaine, and she didn't want me to be around that stuff. Mom and I left walking back home. It was around Christmas time, and granny had just sent me a yellow pullover jacket. I had wanted it for a while, and she sent it to me as a present.

As we were walking down the street, I'm holding my mom up because she is stumbling all over. What stands out most is that I remember she kept lighting cigarettes. Then she would stumble into me and burn my new sweater. After the third or fourth burn hole, I was so frustrated. I told her if she lit another one, I didn't care if she slept in the ditch. She would be walking the rest of the way on her own.

We arrived at James that night only for him and my mom to start arguing. She starts beating and scratching the hell out of him. He wouldn't touch her though, just trying to keep his distance. This night they split ways and she moved to Jacksonville for a little while. I was still going back in forth from James and Tony's, so it was ok in a sense.

This one weekend, Bobby, Heather, and I took his show car to Jacksonville to pick up my mom. He had an Infinity with mirrored windows, tv's everywhere, a banging audio system. Not to mention, it had a paint job that changed Chameleon colors. Nonetheless, we arrived at the gas station a little before mom in Jacksonville. Bobby decided to go in, use the bathroom and get us all something to snack on.

Suddenly, this police officer pulls up behind the car with Heather and me still in it. He approaches and asks where the owner of the vehicle was. Heather informed him; Bobby was in the store bathroom. The police officer then goes into the store, gun in hand. Moments later, customers start running out, panicking. Then minutes passed, the police officer, comes out with Bobby in handcuffs. Me and Heather were so confused.

Because of the way Bobby's car looked, the police officer ran his tag, and then found out he had warrants from when he was younger. Because he threw a brick through the bank window in his hometown. The police officer decided to take him to jail. So now Heather and I were stranded. The officer wouldn't let nobody take the car without a license and mom showing up with no driver's license didn't help the situation. We ended up waiting hours in the parking lot for someone to come pick us up from Georgia.

I started playing football with Pierce County Middle School that year. I loved the game and was good at it too. This was the first time I started to feel proud of myself in life. Mom was at every game to cheer me on. I got to travel around with the school playing games. A fantastic experience all around!

About this time, Tony and I started to bump heads a lot. He didn't want me playing sports anymore. Because it was too time-consuming for them having to keep up with my practices and games. Plus, I was dating a girl from school now and Tony would never let me go hang out with her and her family.

I started getting into fights and getting in trouble at school. Basically, getting paddled during every class. Sometimes two and three times a day; by teachers, the principals, and the coaches too. I think the janitor even whooped my butt a couple times. Not to mention I was getting suspended from school a lot. As time went on me and Caley really started bonding. We were always spending time together: cooking, cleaning, and playing video games. We would cuddle when we were watching movies.

This one incident in seventh grade, these two girls were making fun of me. I had been made fun of or picked on before and always dealt with it accordingly. However, this time, these girls kept telling me I had a tiny penis. In my mind, it wasn't little, and they had never seen it before.

I got tired of hearing their comments and snickering at me for half of the class.

So, I decided to stand up, pull my pants down and shake my penis at the whole class. I got in so much trouble and even dropped some jaws in the process. My teacher whose class this happened in always knew I was a troubled person. Her and a friend would always come to my house with horses. Then we all would go horseback riding and talk about life. She was truly kind to me during these times and tried to get me on the right path in life.

Nonetheless, Tony started whipping me with a belt all the time. It felt like for everything I did. Sometimes he would make life miserable just because he could. If I got suspended from school and it was time to mow the yard. I couldn't use the lawn equipment. I would have to use a swing blade as the old-timers did.

For hours while the other kids were at school I would tend to the yard as punishment. My hands would blister and bleed after. At night when Caley and I washed dishes if Tony found one dirty dish when we finished. Then we would have to wash every dish in the house, that night before bed.

From here, I would start to stay around James' house more and then back to Tonys during school days. I occasionally ended up at Aunt Bea's, where mom was living. James and mom weren't together anymore. Now, he had another girlfriend, Angel, who became like a third mom to me. On the other hand, Bea isn't my aunt but has always been like one to me. She is related to James and is mom's closest friend.

As time went on, James, Angel and I really did grow close. I would go visit mom then come back to their house. One day we were done building this scout mud truck and wanted to test it out quick. However, as were driving down the road, this truck passed us at high speeds. The gust of wind that followed it made James lose control. The scout ended up flipping over and landing on the side.

As the truck hit the ground and started sliding down the road. Glass breaking all over, people flew everywhere inside the cab. I landed on a pointed bar. The two girls with us landed on top of me, pushing the bar through my side. James and his nephew were pulling everyone out of the wreck when they came to me. James noticed my side was torn open and I was bleeding badly. As they were getting me out of the truck, I gained my footing on the ground. Only to stumble over toward the pavement, and then collapse.

What I do remember was coming to my senses and was lying on the ground. Looking up at this beautiful long-haired paramedic cutting off my clothes. After seeing her, I must have passed out again. Because then I woke up in the back of the ambulance. Then again, in the hospital. My side was cut wide open, and my fatty tissues were all hanging out. The doctor shoved it all back in, gave me a bunch of stitches, and then I spent a couple of months recovering.

During recovery, I could really feel the love from my family. I was going to car club meets, car shows with Tony and Bobby. Everyone was helping get by physically. Toward the end of having my stiches in, I ended up moving to dads back in Florida. Then starting school in Narcoossee that following year.

I remember when dad came to pick me up after the wreck. It was him and Uncle Ron, not his brother but his best friend. He was like an uncle to me and Heather. Ron and dad had known each other since eighth grade. Uncle Ron was even at the hospital when both of us kids were born. More into that, He even drove mom to the E.R. while she was in labor with my sister.

However, that night on the way back to Florida, we stopped at the "Nights of Fire" drag races in Bithlo. It was a blast for all three of us. Not to mention one of my best childhood memories I have with my dad and Ron. I was even getting to go to work with them and spend one-on-one time with both that summer. As they worked together, Ron drove semis and dad worked on them. (Story continues after picture).

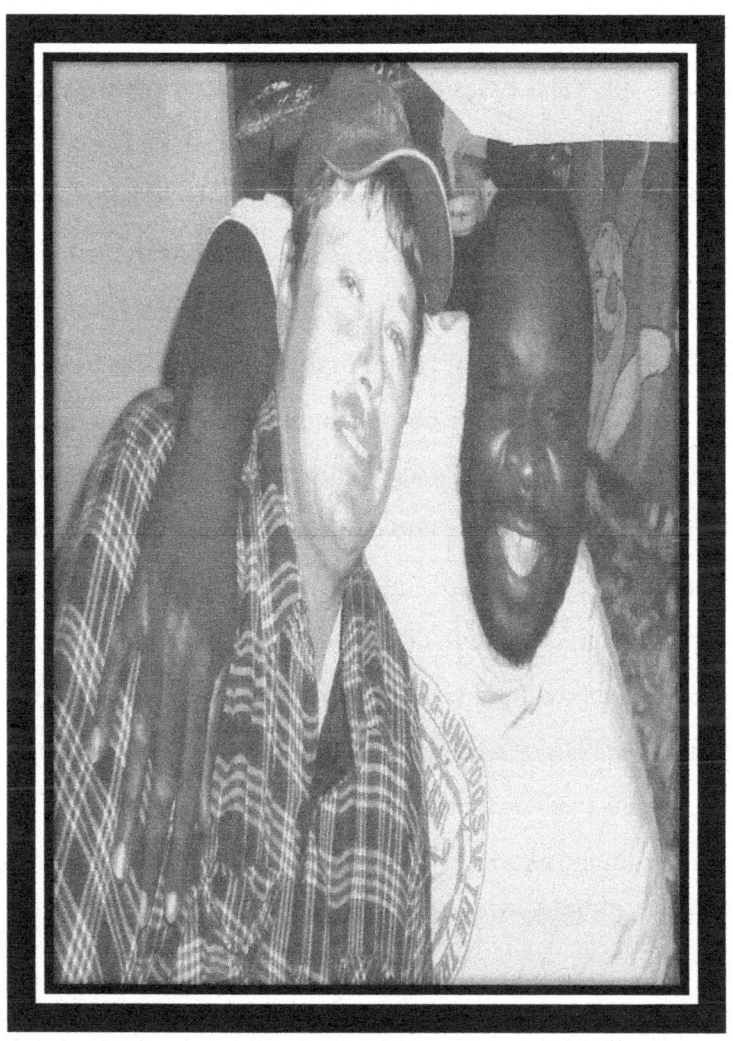

John Sr. & Ron Butler (RIP UNC.)

I can recall this time that summer when dad was working on his friend's car not Ron. This guy started rolling a blunt. I had smoked weed before as you know, so in my mind I was a champion. I kept trying to get the guy to let me hit the blunt without dad knowing. He wouldn't let me until Big John climbed underneath the car to work on it. Then he drops the cigar on the trunk. I picked it up and started hitting it as hard as I can. He would whisper "easy young in this is not regular weed.

Again, I was hard-headed at this point in life and kept hitting it like Mike Tyson. After dad got done fixing the car, we were riding down the road. When everything started spinning in my head, I began vomiting everywhere. Dad didn't even know I was high and was so confused how I got sick suddenly. It wasn't too long after living in Narcoossee that Pam and I weren't getting along. Her and I never really had at these points in time. The more time dad and I would spend together, the meaner it seemed like she would get toward me.

Around the eighth grade, I found myself living back at Tony's house in Blackshear. This time was different though, Tony and Bobby started smoking cocaine. Around these times I got a job at the local car dealership detailing cars after school. Workers from the dealership would always pick me up from school in the newest cars. Which was awesome as a young teen. Tony would then pick me up after work.

Over time he started stopping and getting the drugs on our way home. In no time, Bobby and Tony were smoking cocaine non-stop hiding it from their families. Sometime along the way, I started using it with them when Matty was at work and other times on the car rides home with Tony. Yes, I was smoking cocaine at thirteen. During these times Matty knew nothing about us on drugs and she really worked hard to take care of the family.

I can remember the first time I tried cocaine; it felt like all the stuff I had ever been dealing with just went away instantly. It didn't, though, and never does. That's why it's so hard for people to quit drugs. Once you do these types of narcotics and stop, all the stuff you've been suppressing comes back instantly and then worse.

Whatever the case may be, now I found myself going back and forth from Tony's house to Aunt Bea's where mom was. One place had cocaine, and the other had Marijuana. No one knew what Tony and Bobby were doing. Which meant I couldn't do cocaine or let mom know about it when I was around her. However, she did smoke weed at Aunt Bea's. Her beliefs had always been if I was going to smoke weed, it was at home so she could keep an eye on me. She always said she knew it was going to happen either way.

As a side note, I had a professor tell us a story my brief time in college. His daughter was at a party one night in high school. She was doing drugs and started to overdose. He explained how everyone began to freak out and left her there alone. Sadly, she was not ok and died. The professor wished he could have been around her to maybe save her life. I remember thinking that's what my mom was worried about happening with me and drugs.

Back to my teens years. Once, the cocaine started getting out of hand at Tony's house, him and Matty began to fight all the time. I started staying out at Aunt Bea's house basically full time by now. It was the same school, just a different bus. Not to mention I liked Bea's place more because we always had adventures. One night Aunt Bea, and I was cruising through town in ole red, her old Ford Mustang. She needed some gas money and decided to visit her boyfriend who lived across town to get some cash.

We show up at her boyfriend's house only to find him passed out drunk on the couch. She walked over to check on him. I decided to hit his refrigerator because I had the munchies. Plus, my mouth was dry from all the weed we had been smoking. I'm in the middle of raiding the refrigerator.

When I glance over at her, I notice she is finding money in his socks, that's on his feet. In his underwear, that he was wearing. In the couch cushions, he was sleeping on. In my mind, all I could think was how many times she must have done this. Because by now, this tiny, tiny woman was moving this grown man around, in his sleep, taking his money. Something like you would see a NASCAR pit crew working on a race car during race day.

Another time I went to visit my mom, and she was down the street at her friend Billy's house. We hadn't seen each other in a while for whatever reason. Mom was extremely excited to see me and wondered what I had wanted to do that day. I wanted to go to the river. So, Billy, mom, his daughter, and I loaded up the car and ran a few errands.

Later that day we found ourselves drinking at the river. A couple of hours had passed, and I started to get a headache and was hungry. I kept seeing Billy with this Tylenol bottle and decided to ask him for a couple. Of course, he gave me two pills out of the bottle, and I took them. Come to find out, he had methadone (a strong narcotic), and Tylenol in the same bottle. I had to find out the hard way. Since he was drunk, he must have forgotten about them being in the same bottle together.

I can't tell you how much of what I took as I just popped both pills thinking it was Tylenol and not looking at them. All I can say is when that medicine kicked in, I started vomiting and convulsing, pouring sweat, and freaking out. You could probably say overdosing. I'm guessing it's safe to say everyone was scared to take me to the hospital. Being underage drunk and now overdosing on prescription pain medicine. They decided to put me in the bathtub with cold water running on me and whatever else they could until I snapped out of it. Sometime after this, mom decided it would be best for us to move back to Lake Helen.

"You are tempted in the same way all other human beings are. God is faith-ful. He will not let you be tempted any more than you can take. But when you are tempted, God will give you a way out."-1 Corinthians 10: 12-13

Full verses in appendix

♥ Troubled Teen ♥

Moving to Lake Helen was going to be a good thing. The fresh start mom and I needed. We moved into granny's old house, with Aunt Cynthia and her boyfriend. I started ninth grade at Deland High School and met a ton of people. Pat, Richard, George, and Jason became my closest friends. Later on, would come to meet Andres Abad (Big A) and his cousin Christine.

Pat was older than me and had a car. So, him and I would always be gone somewhere. I would hang out with my older cousin Jason, drinking, fishing, and smoking weed. Mom even thru me a birthday party at Daytona beach that year. We had a hotel room, and my friends came. We smoked good weed, ate decent food, and had a great weekend.

However, Lake Helen had a different feeling this time, granny wasn't living there. She lived across town with her husband, Chuck, on Hontoon Island. It's funny because when mom and I first moved to Lake Helen, Richard wouldn't smoke weed around me. I was fourteen now, and he had to be around nineteen. One day mom and Richard were out back smoking a blunt when I got home from school. He was in shock when mom passed it to me. After that, he and I started to bond.

Then the stories would flow you could say we just connected like best friends or brothers after that. We spent so much time together my aunt would get mad and say we were gay. I never understood it though we weren't sexual in any way. When I wasn't in school, and Richard wasn't working, we would always be hunting or fishing. (Story continues after picture).

Little John, first deer

This one day, me and Richard were fishing; he was on the front of the boat as I was on the back. Richard was in the middle of rolling a blunt. At the same time, he was holding his fishing pole down with his foot. When that bobber sank, he leaned down to grab his fishing pole. I leaned to the same side to see the commotion. As we both leaned toward the edge of the boat. Richard went right over the side into the water, followed by a big splash.

It had to suck for him because it was wintertime, and I couldn't quit laughing at first. He had pants with boots and an oversized camo jacket on. Not to mention, as he fell out of the boat, he tried to grab the trolling motor but failed. However, he did manage to turn it on and point it sideways. But now found himself drowning with all the extra clothes on.

He would tell you it was hard to swim. How he would have to kick off the bottom of the river, then surface on top for a second. Then sink and must do it all over again. It was hard for me to line up with him when he would surface. Eventually, working together, he was able to get back in the boat.

As Richard started to gain his composure, we noticed the bobber floating on top again. He lost his pole, the fish, and the blunt when he fell in. When he saw that bobber, he bent down and grabbed it. Then started pulling the fishing line to retrieve the pole. I have to say he got his fishing rod back, plus the dang fish was still on the hook. Sadly, the blunt didn't make it through the madness.

Another time Richard and I were cruising along the woods during dog season. When this deer jumped out in front of us. Believe me, when I tell you, he jumped out of that moving truck with his rifle. Stumbled as he caught his footing. Somehow managed not to fall and blasted that deer with one shot. If you might have been thinking, was he driving? Yes, he was driving and didn't put the truck in park on his way out. Me being buckled in the passenger seat rolled off and through the bushes.

During these times, my family said I was hanging out with Richard and Jason too much. So, I started spending more time with my buddies from school. One day after school me and George were fishing at the public docks.

When George seen a guy, he knew. They chatted for a minute, and then George and I followed him back to his house. As we go inside this old mobile home, he has drugs of all sorts in there: opium, cocaine, weed, even guns. I had seen drugs before, but this topped the charts in quantity. George ended up leaving with a couple of ounces of cocaine that day.

At first, he was hesitant to let me try it with him. As we were driving back toward our houses, he was cutting up lines on a cd case and snorting them. Eventually letting me try it. I will say either smoking it or snorting it, both ways are super addicting. The next few months that all me and my buddies did was snort cocaine and smoke weed. I was getting in trouble almost every way I could.

Nonetheless, the drugs were getting out of hand and noticeable. At some point I was finding myself back and forth from Hontoon house to the Lake Helen house. This was awesome because Big A lived a couple of streets over from Chuck's house. Big A was a troubled person growing up as well, so we always connected in a brotherly way. He and his mom moved to Hontoon Island from

Miami to live with his uncle, while their home was built there.

Big A's family was from Cuba, and they were completely opposite of my family. However, I always loved being around his family, learning their different beliefs, and eating the good Cuban foods his mom cooked. I was always amused by the way he and his family loved and took care of each other. One thing I learned with his family; they may have been complete opposite from mine, but they still faced hard times the same way we did.

However, me and Big A started smoking weed and skipping school every day. Getting in trouble every way you can think of. I also started dating this girl, and she was a couple of years older than me. Not to mention her family had a lot of money. She would take us to lunch, the beach, shopping, and out on weekends. She would pick me up for school in the mornings and let me drive her car all over. I was still only fourteen at the time.

Her grandparents were extremely strict with her. Which meant she always changed into more revealing clothes in the car on the way to school. I remember she would get down to her bra and a thong to put something else on. All I can say as I drove down the road. The car would be all over the place, with my eyes on her. When I tell you she was beautiful and super smart believe it. I would drop her off at school. Then me and Big A would take the car and skip classes all day.

Around this time, me and mom had received a phone call that my Grandma Irene wasn't doing too well. She didn't have long left to live. I do thank God; mom could get off work to take me to Alabama. Where I was able spend a couple of weeks with grandma before she passed away.

Growing up in Florida, dad's family was always together for holidays and events. They didn't gather anymore after grandma and TJ moved to Alabama with our Aunt Juanita. However, with grandma being sick, everyone was up there including my dad. Not to mention I hadn't seen some of the family in years. (Story continues after picture).

John R. Burnett Sr. and Jr.

It's safe to say TJ had a rough life as well. He is more than a cousin to me; we have always been like brothers. He had been living in Alabama for a while and had started smoking weed as well. So that's all me and him did. Visit grandma during the day at the hospital, and then we would mess around town getting high at night.

Eventually, it was time for me and Tj's dad Chris to board the Greyhound bus and head back to Florida. That was a cool trip and the first time I ever bonded with Uncle Chris. Once mom picked me up in Daytona, we said our good-byes then he continued down to Narcoossee. Within a couple of days of me being back home, grandma sadly passed away. This was a tough time for everyone who knew Irene Burnett.

I'm guessing when mom took me to Alabama to see grandma, it brought back some childhood memories for her. A couple of months after grandma passed away granny decided to sell the Lake Helen house. Mom with Alabama fresh on her mind, decided that she and I would move to Huntsville. We were going to be moving in with her Aunt Joyce. At first, I didn't want to leave. I had all my friends and family I knew in Florida. So be it, not by my choice we loaded the car and were on the way to our next adventure.

Alabama started great like everywhere else. My Aunt Joyce had a huge mansion, the most beautiful house on the block. She lived there with her two sons, and my great granny Ray stayed in an apartment outback. They had a swimming pool, a game room with darts, and a pool table. We would all go out to eat and visit the town, sometimes even bowling. My two cousins and I would ride four-wheelers all over the place. In no time, we were introduced to friends of the family, Matt, and Amy. Incredible people who like to smoke weed as well.

Mom and I were only living there a brief time, and I hadn't smoked weed in what felt like forever. One day, Amy came by, and dropped off a big bag of Marijuana. I couldn't have been more thrilled. It was what I had been missing. My two cousins, Terry, Jerry, and I, we're in the kitchen that night. They were making themselves dinner, and I was rolling a blunt. The boys don't drink or do drugs nor never have. Whatever the case, I rolled the blunt. and headed out the kitchen door into the garage to smoke it.

After you walked into the garage looking straight ahead, the double car doors opened as they usually were. Instantly to the left was the backyard/pool door. That's the door I went out. Outside now, I began lighting the blunt. When I noticed headlights pulling up. I couldn't see the vehicle because I was behind the house at this point. In my mind, Amy and Matt had just left. They must have forgotten something and were returning to get whatever it could be. I quickly decided I would hide behind the door and jump out to scare them.

Once behind the door, I could hear voices coming in the car entrance. It was two men, so I knew right away it wasn't Amy and Matt. Something in my mind told me don't jump out. As the footsteps grew closer, I could now see two people wearing ski masks and holding guns.

As they passed the door I was standing behind, they opened the kitchen door to go inside the house. To my right was the kitchen window. When they opened the door and went inside, I followed them on the outside of the house looking through the window.

Jerry was sitting at the table eating his food. When he looked up from his plate, one guy raised his arm, pointed the gun, and started squeezing the trigger. BOOM, BOOM, BOOM! Every bullet hitting Jerry in the chest, by now trying to stand on his feet. Then as he fell out of the chair face down. BOOM, BOOM, BOOM, more shots to his back! While this was happening, Terry was across the kitchen, still fixing his food. He come running over and punched the shooter in the face. Only to be shot by the second guy, BOOM, BOOM, sending his body tumbling to the ground!

Aunt Joyce and mom heard the commotion and came to see what it was. That's when Aunt Joyce saw Jerry her son getting shot. She then jumped in front of the gun, taking the last bullet to the stomach. When mom saw Aunt Joyce get shot and fall backwards. She ran the other way. Thank God, mom was not seen by the shooters. I knew I had to get out of there and call the police.

The only way out of the yard was back through the garage in front of the shooter's car. The car was still running, and the headlights were on. Plus, I didn't know if anyone was in the car or not. I was terrified! Knowing that my family needed help I had to get the police there.

So, I held the blunt and took off running. I ran and ran until I found a truck to hide under a couple of blocks away. There the blunt was lit, I called the police and told them what had happened. They came full force, ambulances, helicopters, swat team, K-9's, new crews.

Once I made it back to the house which was now a crime scene, the police took mom and me in for questioning. This was a scary time because the detectives were trying to say I shot my family, and they wanted the gun I supposedly used. Even some of my family members treated me poorly thinking the same. Then they wouldn't let me, and my mom talk to each other. Not to mention telling me over and over, I was going to jail for a long time. Eventually, they moved on to other suspects.

Later that night, after we were done being investigated me and mom went to Aunt Joyces daughter's home. We began to smoke joint after joint to calm our nerves. Nobody knew if our aunt and two cousins were going to survive at that point. All three of them were in ICU in critical condition. However back at our cousin's house that night while we were smoking, someone started knocking on the door. Mind you, it's early hours the day after the shooting happened. Scared, something told us not to answer the door and we didn't. Come to find out later it was the people trying to shoot her or find out if she knew anything about the shooting.

Thank God, Aunt Joyce and the boys survived that horrific night, but sadly not without lifelong struggles. Eventually, granny and Chuck came to get me to move back to Florida with them. Shortly after I started having these nightmares of someone trying to shoot me and would bite my lip in my sleep until I bled. Then I would wake up with a mouth full of blood. I don't think I ever really got over this mentally, time just helped.

"We burden not any person, but that which he or she can bear. And whenever you give your word [I.e., Judge between or give evidence, etc.] SAY the TRUTH even if a near relative is concerned and fulfill the covenant of Allah."

- Quran 6:152

Full verse in Appendix.

♥ No Parental Control ♥

By now, granny had sold the house in Lake Helen and was married to Chuck. Now Aunt Cynthia and Richard were living up the street. When we got back from Alabama, I would live between granny's and my aunt's house again. Then I started hanging out around old friends, doing drugs, and getting in trouble a little quicker than I would like to admit.

At this point in life, I wanted nothing to do with school anymore. I had already failed the ninth grade and was at the beginning of starting it all over. When I told my mom that school wasn't for me. She insisted I at least get my GED and I did. The following month Richard would drive me to the college, which I worked on getting my GED. I will honestly say, I was glad she pressured me to do this. Now I was sixteen and was done with school. Oh, what to do.

During this time, I was working with a guy named Larry pumping septic tanks. Larry, granny, and Chuck were constantly telling me about the military. I didn't want any part in it. I didn't even want to hear about it to be honest. At this point in life, I was more focused on girls, drugs, hunting, and fishing. I was working my butt off for long hours and little pay. Spending the little money, I had on drugs and not going anywhere in life.

It wasn't long before Aunt Cynthia, Granny, Chuck and I were arguing every day about something. Maybe not at the time, but now I'm glad I had figures like them in my life. No matter what, they always had my best interest in heart. Not to mention they took care of me when no one had to. On the other hand, they knew nothing about me and my buddies doing drugs all the time. They might have suspected it but never had real proof.

For Instance, one of the adults claimed me on the taxes one year and gave me half the money. However, I ended up buying a half ounce of cocaine with it as soon as I received the money. I got high for a week straight, one of them nights I sat outside snorting line after line of cocaine.

The next morning as the sun came up, I realized I hadn't moved from the seat in over six hours. I decided to go inside the house before anybody woke up. Only to be met at the back door by my aunt, and she was like were you up all night. I had to play it off like I had just woken up and went outside to call Christine. You could tell she always had a gut feeling about something. I would again find myself back and forth from their house to granny and Chuck's during these times.

Chuck is old school, from a different era. So, me and him never agreed on anything. He always treated me good and wanted the best for me. The problem we faced, he was super controlling: his way or the highway sort of speaks. About everything, little or big. It felt like if I tied my shoe wrong, he would lecture me how to do it the right way. Nonetheless, a great grandpa and the only one I have ever really spent time with.

On the other hand, it wasn't that bad staying at their house because Tj could come visit. Not to mention, my friend Big A's house was finished getting built. It was now only six houses down from Chuck's home. As you know, Big A was a troubled child growing up as well, and his teens weren't much better. He was around five feet tall in high school and weighed almost five hundred pounds. Plus, his mom spoiled him, so his house became the new chill spot. We would order food from everywhere, smoke good weed all day, and had parties non-stop. (Story continues after picture).

Tj, and Little John

One-night Big A and his cousin Christine called me. They wanted me to come to stay the night and wouldn't take no for an answer. I was staying at my aunt's house that night and had to get up early for work the next day. In my mind, Christine had already stood me up on a blind date once. Despite that, I ended up going, and I'm glad I did. That was the first night Christine, and I ever really connected. Honestly, I can't tell you who that night was better for. All I can say is that the following day, at work I felt like superman. She was more addicting than any drug I had ever used.

Then things started to get out of hand. Christine and I started dating and running wild. Over time people coming in and out of Big A's got worse and worse. Now Big A, Christine, his mom, and me were selling and using cocaine out of their house. Not to mention his mom was getting a ton of illegal pain pills we would sell too.

One night I went back to granny to get clothes and take a shower. I was met at the door by Chuck who knew I was getting out of control, and he told me if I left not to come back. I informed him he was just slowing me down. Whatever the case, it took five extra minutes to get my stuff, and I was gone. Big A and his mom were very welcoming to me like they had always been.

About this time, Big A's mom still had some old checks from his dad's bank account. The account had been closed for some time since his dad had passed away. However, the next couple of months, Big A and I would go on a shopping spree with his mom everywhere. She wrote every check that was in those books. Back then, cameras at stores were rare, and verifying checks was not as quick as it is today.

We went everywhere for everything you could think of buying. We would buy jewelry, food, clothes, and even bought all new lawn equipment one time. She would make cash advances, sometimes four to five times a day. It is safe to say we thought life was good.

One incident, Big A, his mom, and I were in Walmart buying a shotgun with a check, as the guy went to the back to do Big A mom's paperwork. His mom decides she needs a cigarette and fires one up, right in the middle of Walmart. She was so drunk. Not to mention she never cared about the rules or laws. She used to work in the DA's office in Miami and was super bright in a way.

I can remember as she stood there at the counter smoking that Newport. People were walking by, looking at us like we had lost our minds. Only if they knew we had at that point in life. After buying the shotgun, Big A decided he wanted to shoot it. We couldn't where we lived because the houses were too close together.

While driving home, Big A's mom pulled the car off the side of the road. All three of us got out and I began to put the shotgun shells in the tube. Big A and his mom were nervous to shoot it at first. So, I took it, loaded a bullet in the chamber, and shot a tree on the side of the road. Next, his mom squeezed a round off, and after seeing both of us shoot it. Big A grabbed the shotgun but didn't hold it tight to his shoulder. Then he squeezed that trigger. The gun went off and kicked him like a mull. For the next couple of months, the whole side of his body was bruised.

Sometime after getting the shotgun Big A, me, and a friend of ours decided to steal a bunch of Marijuana. We decided to take his mom's car to hit the lick. Big A was the driver, Bo and I would get out and steal the weed. As we come running down the road to the car, bags of weed in hand. We couldn't see the vehicle because of the tall grass, but we could see smoke coming over the bushes where the car should have been.

We get to the car to find Big A standing there with the hood up and a blown radiator. He informed us how he had gotten bored waiting on us and started cutting donuts. Spinning the car around in circles. Then how it started smoking and leaking fluids everywhere. We beat the mess out of him.

None of us had a driver's licenses. Now, we were in possession of all that weed and broke down on the side of the road. We ended up having to stash the weed in the ditch and calling AAA. We got so lucky with the tow truck driver that showed up. This driver had his wife with him, and they were both drunk off their butts! They had their own bottles of liquor in the tow truck and could barely talk. The driver then informed us there was only room for one extra person in his rig. Taking one look at Big A, he told me and Bo it looked like we were out of luck.

Bo and I ended up persuading him into letting us ride inside the car, on the back of the wrecker. You could tell alcohol played a significant role in him letting us do this. He made it clear we better not get seen. Shoot with him not knowing about all the weed, we understood better than he did. So, Bo and I hopped in the car while the guy was hooking the chains underneath.

Big A quickly grabbed the weed from the ditch and begin to throw us bag after bag. All while the guy wasn't looking. Big A, the tow truck driver, and his wife hopped in the truck; off we went. Us boys couldn't have planned that any better. This guy towed us across two towns to Big A's house, with all the weed we just stole. While me and Bo smoked a blunt in the car and pulling up at the house with Big A getting out wasted.

As time progressed, we were cooking cocaine in the kitchen. People were selling pills, cocaine, and weed out of the garage. All of us at Big A's were strung out on drugs. The sad part was we were all under sixteen and not to mention had dark childhoods. Christine and I became extremely violent toward one another, and our families would try everything to get us to split ways.

One night, she was dropping me off at granny's house. We were arguing while sitting in the car because she had cheated on me. I was pointing my finger at her face.

Suddenly, she bit down on my finger and shook it like a pit bull. I honestly thought she was going to bite it off. As I pulled my hand towards me, with her still latched on. I began to head butt her till she let go. She drove off screaming and crying. I went into the house where I was met by granny at the door.

I started bawling my eyes out. I felt so horrible. Granny quickly gave me medicine to calm me down. Then I informed her the police would be there shortly. To make sure to get me up if I dozed off so I could run. Eventually, I fell asleep, only to be awoken by the police officers poking me with a flashlight. By now, the medicine had kicked in full swing mode, and I kept telling them to come back later. So be it; they took me to the juvenile that night for assault.

It was no time before Christine, and I were back together, but now Big A was in California in a big person camp. His mom was back in Miami with his grandma. So, Christine and I became homeless you could say. We had the choice to go live with our families but not while we were together. In our minds, breaking up wasn't about to happen.

At first living this lifestyle was awesome. I was still working with Larry pumping septic tanks. Christine and I decided to stay at cheap hotels. We kept on using drugs and partying every day. Larry always knew I was a troubled person. Around these times, he really got me to rethinking my ways. He would let me know where I was messing up with my life and talk to me about the military. Larry would always give me words of encouragement and I honestly never felt like he was judging me.

I remember the first run down hotel Christine, and I was staying at. We checked in and dropped our things off. Then me and Christine went to get some food. We couldn't have been gone more than twenty minutes. Only to come back to the room that had been ransacked and all our valuables were stolen. We bounced around the cheap hotels in Deland until we couldn't afford to do it anymore. Take my word, drugs will always hurt you financially, physically and mentally eventually.

After this Christine and I decided to move to Big A's house and live in the backyard. No one was living there, but the water hose, the back porch fan, and the power were still on. We got a tent and did just that. It was about a week or two before the police showed up and ran us off one night. This is where everything Larry said finally kicked in. I couldn't handle living like that anymore. Christine ended up moving to the Keys, with her mom, and I moved to Aunt Debbie's in Narcoossee, for a couple of months.

Aunt Debbie had always fought with her own demons, but I hadn't seen her in a while. This time, she and Uncle Chris were doing well. They both had jobs, were done with the drugs, and had accumulated wonderful things. They did me well during these times. I would go to dad's while they worked during the day and come back home with them at night.

Every day I was all over town on the bicycle. At some point ending up at McDonald's, where Aunt Debbie worked. She would always fix me lunch and get me snacks to take off with me. I can say on or off drugs; Aunt Debbie and Uncle Chris has always tried to do good for me, and I love them both for it.

Like always, the more dad and I were around each other, Pam or I would start showing out. It would just depend on who you asked about the situation. Around this time, I decided I would move down to the Keys, with Christine and her mom. I started doing little jobs around the neighborhood and saving my money for a Greyhound bus ticket. Uncle Chris even helped me where I fell short with money.

As I arrived in the Keys late at night. Christine and her friends were at the bus station excited to see me. After leaving the station, we had to stop at Walgreens to get blunts. Christine and her girlfriend go inside, as the guy and I sat in the car waiting for them. We weren't sitting there for five minutes, when we got swarmed by police. With their guns drawn on us. They started dragging us out of the car. Before I knew it, we were in handcuffs belly to the parking lot pavement.

After ram sacking the car and finding nothing, luckily the weed was at this guy's house. They then informed us someone had called the police. This caller supposedly said we were smoking weed in the parking lot. However, the police officer did tell us how they were already sitting across the street. They were waiting on a drug deal to go down. When they got the call, and how we ruined it for them. I always assumed whoever they were waiting on, knew they were waiting on their drug deal and diverted them to us.

After the rough start, things started going well. We were working for Christine's mom. She had her own lawn business and paid us good money. At this point, the best legal money I have made in my life. We were living in a two-bedroom house with her mom.

It was a tiny place with one bathroom, found in her mom's bedroom. Rent was ridiculously outrageous. Nonetheless it was a new adventure. I was exploring unfamiliar places, eating amazing foods, and living the island life. Not to mention smoking good weed. Eventually, coming to find out Christine and her mom never got along. They fought all the time, about everything.

This one night, we were at Christines friend's house, the same one as before. We were drinking and smoking weed as usual when Christine and I started arguing. I decided to leave walking home and not argue with her anymore. I hadn't been living in the Keys that long and didn't know my way around all too well. I knew this guy lived on one side of the airport, and we lived on the other.

In my mind, the quickest way home was to hop the airport fence, run across the tarmac, jump the other wall, and then be home. Things were going to be smooth in my mind. I skipped the first fence and started walking across the tarmac toward the other side. Then suddenly, security and police start heading towards me fast. I began to run, and it felt quicker than I had ever run before. The part that sucked was our side of the airport was much closer to the water. Not to mention I was wearing a tank top, swim trunks, and flip flops.

Once I jumped the second fence, I found myself in thick mango and briar bushes. Nonetheless, the police or airport security were still chasing me. Now I had to run through the overgrown area as fast as I could, dark with no flashlight. The whole time I was running through there, the thorns and branches were scratching my face, arms, and legs. When I came out the other side, I had scratches everywhere, blood rolling down my face to my feet. I decided to hide in the dumpster close to our house, until it was clear to make it home safely.

Another night we were drinking and arguing like usual. Christine gets mad and breaks the mirror in our bedroom. Then I kept saying I could still see myself because half of it didn't break. She loses her mind and decides to throw the piece that didn't break on my barefoot. I don't think she meant to hit my foot.

Believe me when I tell you, it sliced right through my foot like butter, with blood squirting everywhere. Being drunk didn't help because my blood was thinned out and made the bleeding worse. After my foot healed some, her mom decided it would be best for me to move back to Blackshear with my mom.

Mom was still living back and forth from Bobby's parents and Aunt Bea's house. Now back in Blackshear, everyone was cleaning up their lives or trying at least. Bobby and Tony would occasionally mess up, but nothing like before. We were all scrapping metal to make ends meet. You could say living day to day.

One afternoon I was sitting in the living room watching T.V. with Bobbys mom. When the Army commercial happened to come on. This was funny because Bobby's mom never watched commercials. She would always mute the television during them. However, right before it came on, she went to the bathroom. Now I found myself sitting and watching this one commercial. The Army or military had never sparked my interest before this.

However, something had changed in my head, it was like the television was talking to me directly. I replayed in my mind every time someone tried to talk to me about the military, and how I didn't want to listen before. I found myself thinking about how my life wasn't going anywhere special. Plus, not having money to buy my own necessities in life was taking a toll on me mentally. Later that night Bobby's dad and I talked about me joining the Army. He was a veteran himself.

The next day, I was off to the recruiting station. First, I couldn't join because there was marijuana in my system. I went ahead took the computer test and placed anyway. The recruiter told me how to get urine clean quick and I had to come back.

So be it, the next week, I committed to drinking a gallon of water and pickle juice every day. Then I went back seven days later, successfully passing my urine test. Mom even had to sign the papers for me to join. As I was only seventeen at this point on the timeline. The recruiter gave me three days after the test until I left for basic training.

It was a Friday which gave me one last weekend home. Bobby's parents decided to throw me a big going away party that Friday night. We partied our butts off until Saturday morning. A person couldn't have asked for a better going away party in my mind. Not knowing then, it would be the last weekend I ever spent with Bobby's parents and his Uncle Steve in my life. Rest in Peace Dee, Papa, and Uncle Steve you are deeply missed. At some point in life, each person must take responsibility for their own actions and self-accountability, and this was my turning point.

"Brothers and sisters, God has shown you, his mercy. So, I am asking you to offer up your bodies to him. Don't live any longer the way this world lives. Let your way of thinking be completely changed. Then you will be able to test what God wants for you. His plan is good, pleasing, and perfect."-Romans 12: 1-2

Full verses in appendix

♥ Uncle Sam's Nephew ♥

Joining the Army gave me a good feeling about myself. As I said before I heard stories throughout life and there were a couple of vets at my party. After we all got drunk that night, we even shaved my head bald for the laughs. That following Monday, I said goodbyes to the family. Then I boarded the bus with other people just joining the military. Off we went to Florida, to do initial processing. Then onto basic training in Ft. Jackson, South Carolina.

This was going to be an overnight process. When we arrived in Jacksonville, the first thing was finishing paperwork, then a bunch of briefings. After that on to medical, for shots and physicals. Once the process was completed, the Army personnel let the recruits check into a hotel, close by the station. Not to mention granny was able to visit for the night. It was good on my heart to see her before I left. We spent that night talking about childhood memories, got dinner, and even hung out by the pool. Then the next morning, she watched me swear in, and off I went. Now I was the property of the United States Armed Forces. (Story continues after picture).

Little John, and Glenda

The bus ride to basic training was fun. Each soldier received a meal ticket, and we were able to stop halfway at a Golden Corral. About a mile outside the base the old bus driver passed his hat around for all our contraband. Then he said, "Welcome to hell folks" as we pulled through the gates. You wouldn't believe the stuff inside that ball cap when it came around: drugs, cigarettes, and even loose change.

When we arrived at basic training, people in green cowboy hats and Army uniforms rushed us off the bus. They were called drill sergeants. The screaming and chaos started right away and never stopped. They were yelling at us for everything, making us do exercises for any reason they could find. Sometimes just because you looked funny. All I could think was what did I get myself into? What was I thinking joining this?

The second morning I was there, we were all standing in the chow line. Meanwhile this drill sergeant started yelling about facial hair. He was standing beside me, and my eyes were straightforward. So, I didn't realize he was yelling at me directly. I was thinking shoot somebody messed up in my head, and I quickly came to find out it was me he was confronting. Friends all I will say, he made an example out of me.

Let's just say I had always gotten away with being stubborn in life, until now. Over the next ten weeks, I would endure physical and mental pain like no other. It started with many exercises and briefings to learn the dos and don'ts. At first, exercising was new to me. I could tell that smoking and drugs had taken a toll on my body. Not to mention I even started attending church services when I could.

The one rule I couldn't ever seem to get down was flirting with females. I must have done thousands of pushups for fraternizing with girls. We didn't share living quarters or use bathrooms with them, but we did do ranges and eat at the chow hall together. Training finally started picking up, and eventually my body was too tired to think about flirting anymore.

As weeks progressed training became more intense. By the third week each soldier was issued an M16A2 rifle. If a drill sergeant could get the rifle away from you without you knowing, or you forgot it somewhere. You paid, oh did you pay dearly. With sweat, pain, and a lot of suffering.

Up to this point, I disliked being in service, but now we were getting into the stuff I was interested in— shooting guns, land navigation, survival techniques, the things that ignited my curiosity. I learned how to shoot all the diverse types of weapons; the saw, mark19, m240bravo, AT4, etc. As time went on, and training getting more advanced. We were learning to shoot from moving trucks. learned how to clear houses, hand to hand combat, or you could just say training to become killers.

The scariest training exercises to me were the hand grenade range, the live fire course, and the gas chamber. The feeling from these drills will never leave me. There were hundreds of us soldiers gathered for each of these exercises. Some exercises fun, all exhausting, none you will ever forget. All around once in a lifetime experience.

The first was the grenade range. We were standing in lengthy lines, to which funneled to the ammo sergeant. Once in front of the ammo depot, the ammo sergeant would take your hands put two grenades in them. Then shove them to your chest. Were you must hold them until it was your turn to throw the grenades. I was standing with mine pouring sweat. When this drill sergeant saw me and said, "Burnett, you look nervous. I am not going to have that shit on my range".

In my mind, I kept picturing me dropping the grenades while we were standing in line. Thank God, I didn't or nobody else did that for that matter. It must have felt like years waiting there. Once I finally got to that hole and handed my instructor the second grenade. I checked my surroundings, then pulled that pin, aimed my free arm, and launched that thing as far as I could throw. Then dove down in the bottom of the dirt pit. When that grenade exploded, BOOOOOOOOM! The vibration shook the whole ground, I thought it even my soul. It felt liberating, like I was free.

The next exercise was the live fire; this was a requirement to pass basic. It would happen late at night when we least expected it. The night finally came we trained like every day, ate dinner, took showers, and then started dropping like flies in our bunks. It's safe to say I was starting to sail off with this sweet thing on my yacht. Only to be met by my ship captain, who in real world, was my drill sergeant waking us back up. Within minutes the whole room back up on their feet, full battle-ready, and rifles in hand.

See, we knew it was coming, but we didn't know when. Everyone was still half asleep, grumpy, tired, mad, but couldn't complain or say a word. Off to the range, we went. The course started by us marching miles to the woods. When us soldiers came to this ditch and as we climbed up and over the top of the hill beside it. Bullets began flying right above our heads, by multiple machine guns.

There you must crawl on your back and stomach about two football fields towards the gunfire. As you lay on your back wiggling across that field you can see and hear the tracer rounds buzzing over your head. Meanwhile there is all kinds of explosions going off all over the field. The sounds alone were enough to scare you to death.

After that, we had one more requirement: the gas chamber. This was more mentally challenging than anything. On this day, the drill sergeants let the soldiers overeat. We didn't know why now, and they were shoveling the food in in. All I knew was we weren't ever allowed two and three servings, but today we were. Not to mention the sergeants were way to happy that day. The gas chamber was inside this little run-down building, as we entered this room with our gas masks on already.

The first things I noticed was a box fan and one of the sergeants holding a coffee can with smoke rising from it. He would add another chemical tablet to it and then wave the can in front of the fan. It was already foggy and scorching inside there. This caused the smoke to get thicker and thicker. Not to mention breathing through that gas mask sucked.

There were about fifty troops in this room. Five at a time would approach the door. Take their masks off and say the soldier's creed. We quickly learned the effects of tear gas when we took the masks off and how effectively the mask worked. You could feel the burn on your skin and then down your throat as you broke the seal. While you are saying the creed that air fills your windpipe. Causing you to choke, loose oxygen, and some to lose their minds.

Once the sergeants knew everyone's lungs were filled good. They would open the door and let the five leave, only to move on to the next five. Every time the soldiers would come out of the room they would be coughing, vomiting from all that extra food, and tears rolling down their faces. Every pore on your body would be burning as the sweat rolled down your skin, a horrible feeling. All I could think this is what an insect feels like when it gets spray with poison. By now, basic training was ending. We only had family and graduation day left and they were approaching fast.

Family day was awesome to see the family, but the time went by fast. Mom, granny, Chuck, Aunt Cynthia, and my cousins were able to come visit me. That morning the soldiers arrived early to the graduation field. We hid in the woods in front of the stadiums. Once all our families had arrived and were seated. The commanding general gave a speech.

Then a song "Courtesy of the red, white and blue, begin to play on the speakers by Toby Keith. Suddenly, flash and smoke grenades filled the wood line in front of the stadium. BOOM, flash, BOOM, flash! As hundreds and hundreds of troops poured out of the woods through the smoke. Formed information and began to march to the stadium. It was a sight to see and feel.

After the ceremony, we were allowed to take our families around the base. To show them what we had been doing and learning while we were there. The drill sergeants made it clear that if anyone were caught smoking or drinking, they would fail the course even though we were at the end. Being a smoker and not smoking for ten weeks, I had to sneak a cigarette in. Messing around granny managed to take a picture and told me she would give it to the instructor if I didn't quit. (Story continues after picture).

Glenda, Little John, Chuck

Graduation day followed, then it would be off to Advance Individual Training. I was saying goodbye to my family when this girl came walking up. Her name was Lauren, and she was beautiful. I had seen her around before, and even had to do a few pushups for flirting with her one time. Well, she saw my newborn cousin then wanted to hold him. She met my family, we exchanged smiles for a minute, then off she went.

The crazy thing was we were all shipping off to various places for AIT the next day. When I noticed, Lauren was heading to El Paso, TX, and I was myself. On the plane ride there we managed to sit by each other, we talked, laughed, and flirted the whole way. We really connected, you could say.

She was beautiful, smart, complete opposite of me. No doubt in my mind, an absolute living angel. Once arriving in Texas, she had to go to a different school than me. I didn't get to see her that much during this time. However, we did keep in contact through notes and texting.

Advance Individual Training was like a strict college, but still better than basic training. It was twelve weeks long instead of ten and if you didn't get in trouble and passed all your tests. Everyone could get various kinds of weekend passes. You could get a pass to go around the base a couple of hours a day in your first three weeks. Then four to six weeks, you can get access to go off the base for a couple of hours a day. Then week seven and on, you can get a weekend pass where you left Friday and returned Sunday night.

In no time, I had mastered everything about my weapons system. I would even show the instructors new things or tricks if you wanted to say. We celebrated Thanksgiving that year while I was in AIT. Because there was no time to send thousands of soldiers all over America for one day. The Army had a program about adopting a soldier. Local families would come to pick up two troops for dinner, take them home, feed us, and bring us back later that night.

This was a wonderful experience, me and my battle buddy loaded up, and off we went. The Martinez's welcomed us like they have known us forever. They showed me more love than some of my own blood relatives ever had. Their hospitality and food were a five-star rating across the board if I say so myself. The food was like no other. They had turkey, brisket, every side you could imagine, and the desserts, I mean, it was a magnificent experience all around. We were warned before we left the base, that we were not allowed to consume alcohol under any circumstances.

After dinner, the drinks started to flow. My battle buddy and I were nervous at first, but the family insisted. We gave in quicker than I like to admit. The next thing I knew, our bellies were full, and I was drunk, saying our goodbyes.

The funny once we arrived back at the barracks, eighty percent of the people there was drunk. One guy was wearing a sombrero with his uniform! That's when I knew it was a setup. The instructors must have told us not to drink, and the families that picked us up to give us all we wanted to drink. Believe me when I say we got our butts handed to us that night.

Our Christmas two-week vacation followed, and this was the first time I was able to go back to Florida. By now, Lauren and I were talking every day. Not to mention seeing each other on passes. She decided to come to Florida, with me for a week. Then she would leave to visit her family up North to finish it off. That was one of the best weeks of my life. She and I stayed at the Hilton in

Daytona Beach, went riding four-wheelers, and visiting family all over. After she left, I ran into Christine, and we started talking again.

"Hear all unwelcomed truths, study the writings of others, and write down your own thoughts."-Marcus Aurelius

♥ Sandbox Dramas ♥

After AIT, Lauren and I went on to separate duty stations and our life's continued. Eventually, Christine and I decided we would get married at the courthouse. She was living back in Deland by herself. Moving to Texas would be a fresh start for her. Plus, this meant I could live off base and not be hassled by the sergeants about barrack inspections. The new unit had just returned from a deployment when I arrived. I will say the first six months in the unit were calm. Christine and I were spending a lot of time together; we would go to marriage retreats and ski resorts. (Story continues after picture).

Little John skiing, Ruidoso, New Mexico

What I didn't know during these days, my unit was on a deployment rotation. Which meant they would begin training non-stop for another year-long mission. Training became overwhelming and miserable. The unit would go to the field for two weeks and then come home for a week. Then it was a month in the field, home for a week, and so on until we deployed.

Christine had gotten a job and was working her butt off. Around this time, I could tell she was starting to get lonely. She began meeting single men and women at work. They began to party a lot as most young people did in El Paso. I will say we tried our best at the married lifestyle and there were amazing times. However, the stress got the best of both of us. My neighbors would tell me stories about stuff going on while I was away in the field, but I never wanted to hear or believe them.

A couple of months before my deployment, Christine and I decided it would be a promising idea if Big A moved to El Paso. So, Christine wouldn't be lonely while I was deployed. His mom had passed away, and he had been in a bad car accident. Now found himself paralyzed from the waist down, weighing five hundred and fifty pounds.

So be it, I took leave, and we flew to Florida to pick up Big A. Not to mention visit our families. Christine went to Miami, where he was. Then I went to Deland, to meet her dad and see my family. Her dad and I were supposed to rent the U-Haul to take Big A and his medical equipment back to Texas.

The morning I was supposed to meet her dad, I couldn't find him anywhere. So, I went ahead and rented the U-Haul. On the way back to granny's house to get my stuff, I see her dad's truck coming down the road. I pull to the side of the street, as he comes flying past. Police fast on his trail; lights, and sirens blazing. I whip a U-turn and follow behind the police officers. They finally get him to stop, pulled him out of the car, and handcuffed.

As I started to approach the scene. The officer then pulls a gun and a bottle of rock cocaine out of her dad's truck. As I am trying to speak with the police officer, he informs me that if I didn't leave, I would be arrested too. I knew then I had to get out of there. I couldn't be around that kind of stuff now that I was in the Army.

Once I arrived in Miami to pick up Christine and Big A, with the U-Haul, he was too big to fit in the seat. We decided to unbolt the U-Haul seat. Throw it in the back with his belongings, and then he would sit on the floor in the front. With the motor being inside the cab halfway. This made the plastic piece around the engine inside the cab get extremely warm. Big A couldn't feel the heat because he was paralyzed.

For thirty hours, his leg sat on that plastic cover. When we arrived back home in Texas and finally was able to get Big A out of the U-Haul. We noticed he had a big blister on the leg that was touching the cover. We called the ambulance, and he went to the ER. That wound kept getting worse and worse over the next couple of years, which would lead to him eventually having to lose that leg. (Story continues after picture).

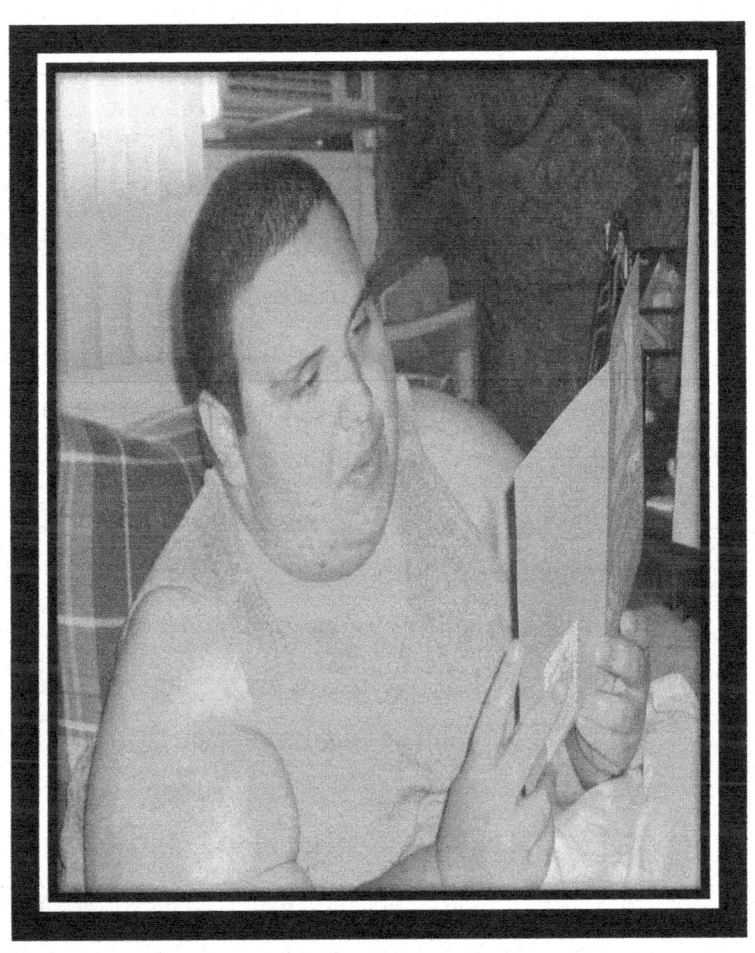

Big A in El paso, Texas.

R.I.P. Brother

Them couple of months before the deployment, besides dealing with the wound on Big A's leg, we had fun times. At first, Big A didn't have nurses to help him. Which meant Christine and I would sponge bathe him, change him when he soiled himself, constantly drain his catheter and prepare his food. Over the months we all really bonded, and it felt like a little family.

On the weekends, all three of us would go to dinner and the movies. We would go shopping and mess around town. Where we lived in El Paso, everything was close to us. This meant we could always let Big A, leave a little before we did in his wheelchair. Then Christine and I would meet him wherever we were going. He didn't have an average wheelchair because of his weight so we were always limited on what we could do together.

It was always something big chair friendly, the park, the movies, or out to go eat. Red Lobster was one of our favorite places to eat. Then no matter what we always went shopping at Walmart after. Sometimes even the mall which was a little further away.

Not to mention We always had the same fantastic waiter at Red Lobster. Over time him and Big A became good friends. On top of that, Christine was twenty-one, and in Texas they had a law. If you're married and one of the parties was of age, and the other was underage you could both drink. Which helped me and Big A when we all wanted to drink.

We would eat, get drunk, then go to the movies. After dinner Big A always tipped the waiter big and with them being close. For free the waiter would always bring us one of every dessert there to carry to the movies. It's funny because we could sneak the desserts into the theater with Big A's wheelchair. Not to mention the waiter would also make us alcoholic beverages to go.

Then deployment came, and it was hard for Christine and me. However, mom, granny, and my little cousin was able to visit me in Texas, before I left overseas, that was good for my heart. We all spent the weekend sightseeing and eating here and there. Just an all-around wonderful time. However, the day came to leave, we said our goodbyes to the families, and begun the next adventure.

As we walked away from each other that day, me and Christine turned around about one hundred feet apart and starred at each other. I could feel the connection being cut then. It sucked because I had always been close to Christine, but in my heart, I knew it was over. It was a weird feeling and heartbreaking in the exact same moment. Then I boarded the bus and took my seat. You could see all the different feelings on each person's face on that bus. Some were excited, some sad, some nervous, and a couple were on a whole other level. However, all I could feel was lost.

When we landed overseas, this was the first time I had ever left the United States. The newness was very unfamiliar and intriguing at the same time. I went from seeing horses to camels, from black widows to giant camel spiders. Instead of grass, it was now sand everywhere. Even the people's language and wardrobes were different. Other than it all being new, the deployment started out great. It was going just like we had trained.

Two months into the mission, I got word Christine had to have hand surgery. It meant she would need help during recovery to take care of Big A. So be it. I took leave and flew home. I was home for the next two weeks, and it just felt different. We made the best out of it and even took a little trip to Carls Bad, New Mexico. Which has a beautiful cave system that goes underground. After she recovered, I headed back overseas.

Once back in the desert, Christine and I started arguing almost every time we talked. Then I started getting random emails from neighbors back in El Paso. Informing me that there was a guy living in my house. How Christine and the guy was having parties there every night. Yes, a twenty-first-century Jody letter. I filed online for a divorce through a lawyer in Texas. Not to mention, currently our platoon sergeant was severely injured. He had to return to the states for recovery. Which was hard on the whole unit, not just me. He was our father figure, and without him around, morale dropped quickly.

I still see that day in my head. When he hit that concrete barrier, he almost tore his face off. As he lay there bleeding from every surface of his body. Trying to talk but gurgling in his blood instead, it became haunting. Something in me broke that day with violence, drama, and people getting hurt. I had been around this stuff my whole life, but now it was starting to play tricks on my mind.

Between divorce proceedings and him getting hurt it was all becoming too much on me mentally. At this point, if I wasn't doing my work, I was arguing with her on the phone. The Army was making me give her almost half of my earnings while we were still married. Since I was across the world, I couldn't physically take pictures of her having sex with this guy. So, the judge didn't want to hear she was sleeping with him without evidence. I was way beyond depressed.

One day I was lying in my bunk feeling low, and Iris stopped by on her way to eat lunch. She stopped by my living quarters to see if I was hungry, or at least to walk with her to the chow hall. Iris was in my platoon, and we worked together on a daily. It was funny because, we were from the same area in Florida, but never had met before. Right from the beginning we always connected on a friend/ co-worker level. Now she found herself going through a divorce as well.

That day though, feeling down and then seeing her. She was shorter with beautiful long hair, thick thighs, and wearing short shorts. Really just out of this world beautiful. It was safe to say food or depression was the last thing on my mind. I don't know who made the first move; just she ended up bent over my bunk, with no bottoms on. I wouldn't say it solved my problems, but she most definitely cured the depression at that moment! Following that Iris and I started messing around here and there for the rest of the deployment.

Nonetheless, my birthday came, and the squad didn't have anything to do but run one drill. After that, a couple of friends and I were supposed to fly to Qatar, for R & R. See, this birthday was special because it was my twenty-first. We couldn't drink in Kuwait because it's a dry country with no alcohol. Qatar, on the other hand, isn't a dry country. Which meant we could get wasted there.

The drill started great. Somewhere in the middle of it, the equipment malfunctions. This metal bar breaks away, busts me in the face, and across my forehead. As other soldiers helped me, I made my way to the medics. Blood pouring out of my nose all over my new uniform. The messed-up part I had been saving that uniform all year just for my birthday to feel fresh all day.

I ended up getting a swollen head, and busted face. Which meant I had to get stitches. However, all I ever have been complimented on in life were my eyes. I didn't want a scar in between them. I begged the doctor not to use stiches. Luckily, he put liquid tape and bandages connecting my skin every couple of hours until the skin took hold on my nose again. Later I would come to find out it was a Traumatic Brain Injury.

Nevertheless, the choice to go home was there, but I knew it wasn't the same. The Army placed me on light duty for the next couple of months. These were adventurous times for me. I was hanging out with Iris here and there. Plus, getting to work in the chow hall. That was a break from what I was used to doing. Every other day, meeting higher-ranking people and the celebrities that came to visit the troops. I was able to meet Ja Rule, Twista, Darrell Worley, and Cheerleaders from all different NFL teams.

By the last month of deployment, nobody cared; we had all lost our minds in some way, shape, or form. Most everybody was sleeping with somebody they shouldn't have been, not following the rules. When we weren't working, we would play music, and the females would give us guys lap dances (with our clothes on). Then the guys would provide the girls with lap dances after.

We started betting on each other, doing crazy stuff. I saw this one guy snort a whole line of black pepper for three hundred dollars. I saw another person drink from someone else's dip spit bottle for almost a thousand. We were making vines or short videos on our down time. One day me and the sergeant were bored and commandeered the ATV. Which we ended up wrecking in the desert. I mean we found fun in some crazy ways during our down times.

It was weird because of how much time us troops spent together; you can't help but grow close to these other servicemembers. When your fellow battle buddies are hurting, upset, or happy, you can sense it. It is hard to explain, but it feels like a love like no other. Deployment would soon be over, and off to America, we went.

I remember our plane landing in the United States. First in Wisconsin to refuel, then onto El Paso. Wisconsin was freezing, and since the whole plane was full of soldiers with guns. It was decided to let us go down the maintenance ramp to smoke cigarettes and see the snow. (Story continues after picture).

Glenda, Little John, and Stephanie

Then onto El Paso, getting off that airplane, smelling that fresh air, and seeing our families. It was the best feeling of home I ever had. It was sad and great at the same time. Christine and I were no longer together, but mom and granny came to welcome me home. It was exactly what my heart needed.

After turning weapons in, debriefings, and getting checked into the barracks. The unit was free to go for the weekend. So, I spent the next couple of days with the family sightseeing and shopping. It was an exciting time. Once granny and mom went back home. I found myself single and now living in the barracks. I knew all the people there, so the parting begun. We would all go clubbing every night and run up large bar tabs together, life was going well.

Until one day, one of our best sergeants committed suicide. This took a toll on me personally because I was the last person he was with. He drove me home because I was drunk. Something was bothering him, and he kept trying to talk to me about it. But I couldn't stop vomiting. As he dropped me off, I told him we could talk in the morning, but morning didn't come for him. He went home and shot himself. After that I started drinking heavily to mask the pain. It really was a horrible feeling.

One night my friend Mo and I were clubbing. After closing time, we found ourselves back at the hotel, outside smoking cigarettes. It had to be around three in the morning when Mo started to hear these girls talking. Low and behold, four beautiful women came up to us! One asked if we had a lighter, and of course, I did. Besides smoking, Grandma Irene had always told me to have a lighter for survival reasons. Thank you, grandma, it paid off! Come to find out, they were strippers just getting off work.

These young women were super smart and beautiful. They would come to El Paso from Oklahoma for three months a year to work the strip clubs there. Then take the rest of the year off back in Oklahoma with all the money they would make. Mo and I spent every day with these girls for the next two weeks. Having a blast probably getting into more trouble than we should have.

However, with only a brief time left on my contract, I had saved up my leave, and the first sergeant knew I was partying a lot. He told me to go ahead and take terminal leave before I found myself in trouble. The day before I was leaving to come back to Florida and saying goodbye to the Army life. Mo and the group threw me a going-away party! That was the first time I had smoked weed since going into the service. I got so high, and even hooked up with my female sergeant that night.

During Army out-processing, I had been warned that there would be people back home up to the same sad things. How not to fall into any of these old patterns. Oh, there was, and I ran into all of them. After I was officially being released, I headed to grannies in Florida.

Around this time, I ran into my old friend Pat from High School. We decided to take a road trip to Georgia to see my mom and then to Tennessee to see an old girlfriend. We partied hard in Tennessee and started using cocaine on top of smoking weed. It was a non-stop party from the time we left Florida, until a week later when we got back off the trip.

After that weekend, Me and Pat kept partying in Florida, doing the same things more and more. One night in general, we partied into the early morning. Being to intoxicate to drive, I asked Pat if he would drive me home in my car. However, he had booty on his mind and wanted to go with his girlfriend. My only choice was to have granny meet me in town.

Knowing she couldn't find her way through the woods that late. I started the car up and headed towards town. Once out of the woods and on the hardtop, blue lights appeared in the rearview mirror. I quickly decided not tonight and floored the gas pedal. As I gained speed and blew through the red lights, the police had to slow down at them. This gave me the time I needed to pull ahead.

As I turned into the parking lot where granny was waiting, I threw the drugs out of my window. I parked the car and threw the keys on the floorboard. Then I hopped into granny's car who was sitting there waiting patiently. As I hop in her car then police come flying by us and continued down the road. We ended up leaving my car in the parking lot, and granny drove me home.

As she and I pulled out of the parking lot, I made her stop. hopped out and grab the weed. The bag had opened, and the weed went everywhere. Now I found myself walking around the parking lot picking up the buds.

Finding myself back on the same path of destruction. Deland wasn't the place for me currently.

"Life is a circle of happiness, sadness, hard times, and Goodtimes. If you are going through hard times have faith good times are on the way." -Buddha

♥ Answered Prayers ♥

Something inside my soul was pushing me to go see my dad. After the narrow escape with police, I decided it was time to visit Saint Cloud. I arrived at dad's house and started pounding on the door with excitement. It had been a while since I had seen everyone. When the door swung open, my stepmom was standing in the doorway excited to see me.

Right over her shoulder was the most gorgeous girl I had ever seen in my life. It was my stepsister's friend Kehana. She had long dark hair, a smile that lit the room up, and when she turned around, a butt that was so perfect. In no time, me and her was spending every day together, going to water parks, hanging out with my stepsister and her boyfriend, or sometimes visiting my granny.

This one night, Kehana and Haley wanted me to meet them at this nightclub. However, on the way there I was pulled over for loud music. Not to mention while I was smoking a blunt. When I rolled my window down, and that smoke hit the officer in the face. He quickly went from a smile, to get out of the car. This was not good for me or my stepbrother who was on probation. Eventually, I ended up paying over thousand dollars in fines and had to do fifty community service hours. Endless urinalysis tests and probation for six months.

During all that, Kehana and I started dating and moved into our first apartment together. We both made good money and could do whatever our hearts desired. Eventually, we bought a boat and started fishing all the time. We would go camping, travel all over, cook together, hang out with our families, really everything you can think of. We became best friends in my eyes. This was an all-around exciting time in my life.

Around this time, my mental and physical health started declining. Life and Karma were finally catching up with me. I started right away going to the V.A. for treatments. They diagnosed me with a TBI, PTSD, maniac depression, anxiety, sleeping disorder, etc. Then the pills for each diagnoses followed, and then the doctors sent me on my way. During these days, Kehana and I would have little arguments like an average couple. Overall, we were still close.

I began using the G.I. bill to attend college, and Kehana wanted to go to school as well. This would have cost her mom a bunch of money they didn't have. That's when she and I decided to get married. So, she would get financial aid. Our wedding was a small one on Daytona Beach. I married my best friend, and to me she was always a gift from God. That day more than ever though.

We had a tiki bar at the resort, so everyone there was drinking before and after the ceremony. Then we had a small gathering at the steak house after. Really just a blessed night all around. Getting married to Kehana was the best thing I could have done. (Story continues after picture).

Little Johns 2nd wedding

One weekend, my mom was visiting us in Deland. Mom and I were on the front porch smoking a joint, when Kehana came out holding a pregnancy test. Her face was bright red, with a smile. She looked at us and said, "I think I'm pregnant". As her beautiful eyes were watering up. We had both been wanting a baby for a while.

I exploded with excitement, thinking I was the man, hugging and kissing her! Not to mention, my eyes even started watering up. Mom was super excited, crying, and hugging us both. Later that night, Kehana wanted to know if she really was pregnant. Her poor mind had to be all over the place. She and I decided to go to the emergency room to get checked out.

The nurse began putting the IV in Kehana's arm. She missed her vein and was moving the needle around inside, trying to find it. For some reason, being high when I saw this, it made me get light-headed and dizzy. I asked the nurse to open a window.

I'm guessing there wasn't any. Because the next thing I know, I'm in the hospital bed, getting checked by doctors and nurses. Eating a sandwich and drinking a juice box. Meanwhile Kehana is standing in the corner in worry mode. After that, the next nine months were amazing to see her grow and glow.

This one weekend her mom and stepdad came to visit us in Deland. Her stepdad and I were coming back from night fishing in Edgewater. When I pulled up to the store, to grab some ice for the fish we caught. I opened the car door and stepped out.

Quickly noticing a big bag of cocaine laying on the parking lot. I starred at it and intuitively knew what it was. The bag was run over multiple times, and the powder was all over the outside of the bag. So, I told her stepdad to grab it while I went inside to get the ice. He did, and when I got back, he was clearing his nose.

We went straight home, and I told Kehana we found the cocaine and how tempting it was to try. The following week on Facetime, her mom would tell us how her stepdad caught a sinus infection, but we knew what it was from. For me things were different now that I was married, and Kehana was pregnant. The same things were no longer fun to me. I was finally getting the one thing I had ever really wanted in life: a family. Oh, How I had prayed for this my whole life.

One afternoon I was outside smoking. When I come walking inside to find Kehana standing in the kitchen looking funny. She said I think my water just broke as she felt her panties. The only thing she wanted was to take a shower before we left. She was so calm and collected at this point.

On the other hand, I was pacing the floors, sweating, nervous, and panicking. You would've thought I was going into labor. She would have to remind me what we needed to take, as I loaded the car. Off to the hospital we went; Labor was a prolonged process. She tried her hardest to do it naturally. We would walk the hallways, and she would stretch. I want to say after twenty-plus hours, the doctors wanted her to try the epidural, and it was a successful labor after that.

Grayson was our only child, so this was all new to us. I became extremely nervous with him. I had seen the dangers in this world firsthand and had already been diagnosed with all kinds of mental problems. It all became terrifying. It was safe to say it became hard dealing with the things that would go through my mind. Kehana understood and always showed me love during these times. By now I was working for her brother cleaning carpets. Not to mention, making good money and didn't work long hours. Which meant I could be home more with Kehana and Gray boy.

I remember this one job I arrived at and found the homeowner rolling a blunt out front. The next thing I know, I'm smoking weed with this guy. Then we're in the house, and he is showing me all kinds of cool things. He even fed me lunch. About three hours later, Kehana's brother calls me wondering why I was still there. Heck, I haven't even started cleaning the house at this point.

As time went on, the VA kept increasing my medicine more and more. My physical and mental health was declining rapidly, and no one could tell us why. Just kept giving me more medicine. By now I couldn't do crowds of people, which cause me to quit college. As I kept getting sicker and sicker, losing weight rapidly, it became harder to stand up, and becoming blind in one eye. I just started thinking I'm dying and became mean to the people I loved most.

With my health declining I could no longer physically do what I used to. My looks changed dramatically, and I started noticing how people would look at me. It really hurt inside and out. In no time I begin to hate people, myself, and life in general. The sicker I became, the easier it was for me to be mean. People would call me every horrible name you could think of. Nobody wanted to be around me anymore which I can't blame. This destroyed me on so many levels I had always been a people's person.

Me and Kehana were now living in Inverness around her family. When she finally started to grow apart from me. I was at the VA what seemed like every day. My liver started acting up from all the medicine the doctors had me taking. Then the doctor tells me I needed a liver biopsy and set up the appointment. (Story continues after picture).

A Father & Son's love

The month before the appointment was pure madness in my head. Something kept telling me, don't do this, don't do this surgery. I would lay awake at night crying with horrible stomach aches thinking about it. We decided that Kehana, Grayson, and I would stay at grannies in Deland, for my recovery.

The day came; we left the little one with my aunt. Me, Kehana, and granny headed to Gainesville, for my procedure. It was supposed to be an in-and-out type of surgery. Once there, they got me in the back and started preparing me for surgery. The surgeon reads my chart and tells the nurse he would like to see my Rheumatoid Arthritis doctor before he does anything.

My RA doctor shows up, and the doctors began to argue. Over if I needed the procedure or not. One said I did, and the other one said I didn't. Nonetheless the surgeon is mad at this point, turns to me, and then rolls me on my side. He then sticks the numbing needle in my ribs. Immediately after grabs the ultrasound machine, finds my liver. Stabs the biopsy probe through my ribs, and into my liver.

First, I will say he gave the medicine no time to kick in and do its job efficiently. I felt every bit of it. Second, instead of getting tissue off the top of my liver to test. He stabbed me right through my liver. Through the top and out of the bottom. Which I didn't know at the time. After the surgery, I was sent back to grannies for recovery to begin. That night back at the house, I became so sick. I was throwing up blood and pouring sweating. So Kehana and granny had me rushed to the hospital in Daytona.

The hospital tells us it is a kidney stone, and I would be sick until I passed them. It was unfortunate that this happened right after my surgery and sent me back home with medicine. Something still wasn't right. I was super sick at this point. Kehana and granny wanted me to go back to the hospital, but I had enough of life. Now it felt like I was being attacked and went straight into survivor mode.

In my heart, I felt like I was dying and knew my body was finally wearing down. Watching Kehana scared and feeling like I was being attacked by everyone. I just flipped out and told everyone there if they didn't leave me alone, I was going to kill them all. Right after that they decided to call the police on me. Now I knew I was going to die. The police officers were going to kill me in my mind. I sure wasn't sticking around to talk to them or find out. Quickly I decided to hop in the car and run.

While driving, I kept vomiting blood all over me and the car. Finally making it to my house in Inverness, where I felt safe. In my mind if the police wanted me, they would have to come for me at this point. That was the day Kehana, and my son left. They moved across the state, and I wasn't allowed to see them. I was home for a couple of days, steadily bleeding out internally. Just smoking weed and waiting to me my maker. When Heather shows up, with my nieces.

Finally, I was too weak to keep going and rushed back to the hospital. However, it was in Inverness this time not Daytona. This is where I found out the VA messed up during the surgery. The VA messed up so bad that this hospital wouldn't even treat me for lawsuit purposes. From there they transported me back to the VA in Gainsville, Florida, in a hurry.

These were terrifying times for me. Not to mention this was the hospital that jacked me up in the first place. Plus, not seeing Grayson and Kehana was taken a toll on me mentally. There I spent the next few weeks in ICU getting blood transfusions and getting fixed to an extent. I had four different IV sites with eleven bags of various fluids and medicine going into me at one point.

One day this man came to visit me while I was in recovery. He was bald with a white beard. He told me some things and how to turn to God. How I would see and spend time with my son again. Not to seek revenge or do anything dumb when I was released from the hospital. How things would work for me, then smiled and went on his way. I had never seen him before or after that. Later, I asked the nurses, what that man's name was that had visited me. They swore nobody was in the room or had been in there.

Nonetheless after getting out of the hospital. I was staying at home alone and was giving myself shots in the stomach every day. I had always hated needles because they made me feel faint. So, I would have to lay on the bed and clean the area with an alcohol pad. Every time I stuck that needle in my stomach, I would pass out. When I would come to, the needle would be hanging out of my stomach. Then I would have to get it out and go on my way. As time went on things got hard for me by myself. So, I asked Aunt Pat to move in with her.

"We did not wrong them, rather they wronged themselves. When God (Allah in Islam) does seize the towns (or people) immersed in wrongdoing, His seizure is painful and horrific."- Quran 11: 101-102

(Full verses in appendix)

♥ Why Me ♥

Unable to care for myself completely Aunt Pat opened her house and made me feel right at home. Throughout life, Aunt Pat and Uncle Pete has always been good to me. Sadly, Uncle Pete had passed away in my teen years. God, please watch over his soul for me. Now it was just Aunt Pat and my cousin Jason living there. I really couldn't have made it without them during these tough times. I was always sick, depressed, and in pain. Constantly in and out of the hospital with my liver messing up.

It wasn't long before I met back up with Big A. He was living in a nursing home in Deland. I was still weak at this point, down to one hundred and eight pounds from one hundred-ninety. Not to mention, I was now taking prescribed pain pills on top of all the other medicines. It had been two months since I had seen Grayson, and it was mentally taking a toll on me. This was the only time I had ever been away from him.

On top of dealing with all this, then I had to start going to the pain doctor. With the opioid epidemic happening. That was a nightmare. I remember the first and last visit to the pain clinic. The doctor did what he was supposed to. I took and passed my drug urinalysis test. He then gave me my prescription and off I went to the pharmacy.

The same place I always filled my medications. However, the lady working takes one look at me, and notices I had lost a lot of weight. She even asked me what happened to me, but I didn't want to converse about life. I really hated interacting with people at this point. Then she informs me they didn't have that kind of medicine. She told me she would fill everything else, and I could come back in a couple of days to get the pain medicine. I showed up there three different days and received the same response.

Nonetheless, now the medicine from the hospital had run out and I found myself in serious pain. As there still was a hole through my liver. I decided to take my prescription to the Publix in town. Once, I got to the counter, and the pharmacist looked at my prescription. Then looks me up and down. Proceeds to inform me she couldn't fill my medicine. I asked her, "why not"?

I was curious now with this being the second place. She then tells me it was because I looked strung out on drugs. Shocked, I'm like, what! Nevertheless, she then informs me by law, she can do this. With everyone in line now looking at me. Embarrassed, I held in my anger and walked away. I was used to showing out in these situations, but it would have only made her look right in this case.

After this incident I decided I wasn't going through that kind of embarrassment anymore. I started getting my pain medicine from dealers or off the streets if you want to say. Not to mention, with Big A being overweight the doctors prescribed him all kinds of narcotics. However, he never took them just kept them. Then he would sell the medicine to the nurses at his home or give them to me.

During this time, I started going to the cancer center for iron treatments as well. I remember seeing people of all ages getting various kinds of treatments there. With my depression already high this would weigh heavy on me mentally. What really helped me get by was Caley, Matty and Tony decided to move to Florida.

They moved in with Heather and her kids. I hadn't seen them since joining the Army and being around them just brought back good memories. In no time, me and Caley were spending a lot of time together and then started dating. Not to long after, I started getting to spend time with Grayson again. Which lifted my spirits even more. (Story continues after picture).

Little John, and Gray after three
months

I eventually rented a mobile home in Lake County for me, Caley and her kids. Plus, Gray boy was getting to come over on the weekends. Life started to feel good again for me. Sadly, by then I had a pill addiction and didn't have the physical strength to do what my mind wanted to. Not by choice but really by choice.

Nonetheless, it was becoming a problem. My mom would come down and help me get by physically and mentally. Then occasionally, we would go spend time in Georgia with her for a change of scenery. After me and Caley begin popping pills all the time, money started getting tight. Neither one of us worked and were constantly around each other. Which would lead to us arguing. When the tension would get bad between us, she would always go back to her boyfriend in Oklahoma. Then eventually make her way back to our house in Lake County.

One of these times Florida, was hit by a hurricane which isn't unusual. However, the chain reaction it sparked was. Me and Caley were outside cleaning the debris to blow off steam. See it was my birthday and the power was out, and nowhere to go. I decided to build a bonfire and burn all the fallen debris.

The wind picks up making the fire grow even bigger. Then starts blowing the embers toward the neighbor's house. The next thing I know he comes outside mad and goes to get his yard tools. Proceeds to climbing up his roof and then started cleaning the debris off.

I go on with my business. Next thing I see the fire truck and ambulance coming. Shortly followed by a helicopter arriving at his house. In my mind, I'm thinking the neighbor called because of the fire. Come to find out, the man fell through his roof and was impaled in the chest. Ending with him being airlifted to the hospital. Sadly, him never making it home it home.

Nonetheless, buying the pain pills off the street was getting expensive. Me and Caley was arguing all the time. Then when we were out of medicine, I would have to deal with withdrawals: chills, sweating, mood swings, and vomiting nonstop. When Grayson would visit, I couldn't afford to do the fun things he wanted to do. That's when I decided it was time to quit the medicine. I finally had to accept being disabled and blind in one eye wasn't going to change. Then I needed to learn to live life without masking my pain and quit blaming my problems on everyone else.

One day Caley and I were arguing as usual by now. I hadn't been taking pills and was sick from withdrawals. Big A calls me from the hospital in trouble. He had started smoking meth with one of the nurses at the home. Then he somehow got a taser in there. Apparently, he was high and fell asleep with his pipe in his hand.

A nurse who wasn't on drugs happened to come in his room. She seen the pipe and tried to take it from him. Then he woke up startled and tasered her. I mean, he fried her butt. They couldn't send him to jail because of how many medical conditions he had. Not to mention how big he was. The home had to send him to Halifax Behavioral hospital in Daytona to await his fate.

That day between life, having the withdrawals, arguing with Caley, and dealing with Big A. I lost my mind in a sense. In between all that I popped a hundred milligrams of morphine. When that pill took effect on me, all the anger I was holding in came out. I started to drink on top of taking the medicine. Later that night as we're arguing

I go outside, hop in my SUV, and start ramming Caley's car. Then take off down the road. Next thing I know, I am surrounded by police in Walmart parking lot. With their guns drawn, and lasers all over my chest.

As the police spoke to me on the PA system; I remembered having a joint in my ear and decided it was a suitable time to smoke it. After a half hour stand-off, the pills, alcohol, and weed were in full effect. Finally, the police were able to get me in handcuffs. Then I spent the next month in the behavioral hospital getting treatments. This was exactly what I needed, a mini vacation from the madness. It gave me time to collect my thoughts and see what changes I needed to make in life.

After I was released, Caley come to bring me home. It was an amazing feeling to hear her voice and see that beautiful face. Once arriving back home, I found out Big A had passed away while I was in there. The sad part, we were at the same hospital when he died and neither of us had a clue. He wrote to me on the PlayStation wondering why I hadn't visited or called him. After losing my closet friend I decided I was done with the pills. Me and Caley decided our relationship wasn't working and split ways. She moved to Oklahoma for the last time. After Caley left, I packed up a few important items. Left the rest and moved to Saint Cloud, not to look back.

This time moving to Saint Cloud, I took a personal oath to better myself in all areas of my life. I moved back to Aunt Debbie's house and begin doing just that. At first, moving there was tough. The depression would kick back in and a sense of failure. I didn't like myself and still had to learn to quit blaming others for my problems.

However, at least I was on the right path, saving money, making doctor appointments at the V.A. again. I started exercising and took a deeper look at what religion meant to me personally. I was finally able to do more fun things with Grayson when we can get together. Started spending more quality time with my mom, dad, and stepmom. Not to mention, trying to visit granny as much as I can. I even met an intelligent goddess, who this world had sadly turned deceitful and devious. I will say she helped me see the path I needed to take in life crystal-clear.

My dad's brothers, passed away within months of each other one year. Uncle Rick passed away knowing he was terminally ill and never told any of us anything. After they passed away, it seemed to ignite something in the rest of the family. Since then, everyone has been gathering and talking more. It sad to say we learned the hard way tomorrow is never promised.

As I mentioned before, mine and Grayson relationship has kept growing in ways, I can only give credit to God for. It has been such a joy for me to watch him grow. We now do things like fishing, zoos, play mini golf all over Florida, I go to his football games, or we play video games together. We try to visit granny and mom as often as we can. Which he loves to do. (Story continues after picture).

Heather, Little John, Stephanie, and Glenda

Since making life changes and moving back to Saint Cloud, God has blessed me in so many ways. One being quality time with my family in general. Me, Aunt Debbie and Uncle Chris went to North Carolina to visit TJ and his family. It is great knowing how far he has come in life. He has an amazing family and works hard every day take care of their needs.

I have prayed my whole life to take a road trip with my dad, and God has blessed me with three in one year. The first one was to see Aunt Juanita for her husband's birthday. This was one of the most incredible trips of my life. Dad's sisters were all there. TJ and his family came and stayed. Even Aunt Juanita's son Jimmy was there, I hadn't seen him since I was a young. We all spent the next couple of days hanging out, sightseeing, and eating tasty food.

I haven't been there since 2005, when grandma was sick. After grandma was cremated half of the ashes were buried in Alabama, and the other half in Ohio with Papa James. Before we all said our goodbyes and went our separate ways. We spent the day cleaning the cemetery where grandma and cousin Brenda are buried. We planned our next trip up there for that Thanksgiving and headed out. After I got back to Florida, I received news from momma that our Aunt Joyce, in Alabama during my teenage years, had passed away. These were sad times for our family. With the Lord's help and knowing we will see her again. We were able to pull through the tough times.

A month later, dad come over to tell me the Burnett's in Ohio were having a family reunion that year, 2020. He and I were supposed to go the year before but couldn't because of COVID19 lockdowns. So, the reunion was canceled. However, 2021, we had a go. July rolled around, and it was time to head out. My dad, stepmom, and I set off once again.

It was a sixteen-hour drive straight through. We laughed, sang songs, and enjoyed the scenery. Which was breathtakingly beautiful. We even went through a couple of tunnels, through the mountains, and seen beautiful bodies of water. Not to mention diverse types of bridges, and how we almost got run off the mountain by another car.

I had never been to Ohio; these places were new to me. I felt like a kid all over again. That afternoon we arrived, checked into the hotel, ate, and took showers. Dad was telling us the county he grew up in, always had a fair the last weekend of July. How he hadn't been in forty years.

Low and behold, the fair was up and running as we drove into town. You could see my dad's face glowing. After we showered, it was decided to go check out the fair. That night, they were hosting a truck and tractor pull. Which is my dad's favorite thing to watch. To be honest there was some nice old Fords, and they were fun to watch and hear.

The next morning, we made it to the reunion. I met a bunch of great family members. However, I met a couple of them before on the phone when Uncle Rick was alive. Now I could put faces with their voices. They reminded me just like my dad's side of the family, which I did know growing up around in Florida.

The family history I got to learn, see, hear, and feel on this trip was more than I could have ask for. It was an all-around extraordinary experience. We visited the grave site, put flowers and nick-nacks down. This was a short trip but the most fun I have had with my dad and my stepmom. I thank God for it too!

I don't know what the rest of life has in store for me yet, as I'm only going to be 33 this year. I want to thank God Almighty, for not giving up on me along the way, even though I wanted to give up on myself. After writing this journal, I'm leaving the past, and moving into the present. All I can hope and have faith for, is my life doesn't end how it started for everyone involved. I have always said I made it through life by myself. That is such a wrong statement, it really took a village to raise me. So, thank you with all my heart to everyone who had a hand in me getting here today. To the ones that feel I have wronged them, I sincerely apologize to you. To those who have done me wrong in life. I pray the best of luck upon you! To be continued.

Little John, Pam, and John Sr.

"Every sin and every evil word spoken against God, or the Son will be forgiven. But speaking evil things against the Holy Spirit will not be forgiven now or in the days to come." Matthew 12: 31-32

(Full verses in the appendix.)

(P.S.)

♥ Autumn of Life ♥

With time I have met, been hospitalized, and truly connected with people society has labeled: crazy, dangerous, nasty, evil, etc. Majority of the time they had the biggest hearts. Sadly, no one wanted to take the time to understand them and the terrible things they have faced. Sometimes we don't know what a person is going through. They could laugh on the outside and be dying on the inside. Overall, I have learned to try to be a nice person and show everyone respect. Now when evil or drama is upon me, I do my best to walk away when I can. Letting God and the Holy Spirit take out vengeance for me.

Through all the negative things I have faced in life, it was always easier for me to blame everyone else for my mistakes. However, I have also learned with time, there is no one to blame for our personal life choices but ourselves. Every one of us is dealing with horrible things in life and learning as we go. It is up to us as individuals to decide which paths we will take, after the hard times we may have faced.

Me personally, I can only try to fix where I messed up in life and let go of what can't be undone. Life has taught me it is hard to enjoy the good things God blesses us with, when I'm holding in so much negativity, pain, and hate. Since discovering more love for God and myself, my perspective on life has changed. I have realized life is how each of us choose to view it.

These past few years have been amazing to see Gods firsthand work in my family's life's. I want to personally thank the First Baptist Church of Barberville, Florida, and their pastor for helping some of my family transition from the dark. On occasion, you will find my entire family in attendance there. Let me tell you, seeing us all in a church is a miracle by itself.

As for me, I still have a lot to work on, but everyday strive to be better than I was the day before. I have learned for me to be happy in life it starts with myself and finding the balance between good and bad. Some ways I find balance are praying to God, talking to someone, listening to music, meditating, and getting in touch with nature. I started paying attention to what goes into my mind through television, social media, music, my choice of friends, basically a lot less negativity. When you don't think about the dreadful things in life constantly, you will find it easier to deal with life's problems when they arise.

If you ever find yourself wanting to give up on life. Just know, it is ok to seek help and not feel ashamed. Trying to mask the pain in any way will only cause you further damage. It's also good to know when it seems like everything is against you God isn't. If we like it or not, we are all in this world together. God loves each of us no matter our, race, location, or background. When things are going well in life, help someone else in need. Most importantly never judge a book by its cover. Remember our judgements or words can effect a person's life if we know it or not.

Bottom line, if you are unhappy with your own life or find yourself on the wrong path in life. You chose that not God, the devil, or anyone else for the matter. Each day is a new beginning for each of us. A chance to change the person we were the day before. An opportunity to spread love over hate, joy over misery, light over darkness and truth over lies. My life has been full of adventures, good and bad, ups and downs. Some can be spoken about some cannot, and I thank God for each of those days.

Hopefully everyone will have a better understanding life doesn't always go as we planned. But will always go according to God's plan. Just keep rolling with the tide. Never giving up on yourself, no matter who else might forsake you. If you ever find fear holding you back in life. Get out of your head, seek help if needed, and go put your marks on the world in the greatest ways. For now, all I will ask you is, what's keeping you from living your most righteous life?

Basic Training Peer Reviews vs. Active Army Awards

PERFORMANCE COUNSELING RECORDS
See Privacy Act statement on front of this form.
This form will be destroyed when no longer required.

DATE: 01 NOV 07   Name, Grade, Signature of Counselor: Flores, ⬛⬛⬛ SSG

CIRCUMSTANCES AND SUMMARY (Include the expected standards and how the standards were not met)

- you need to establish more discipline on yourself. You lack alot of doing the right thing when nobody is watching.

- You need practice silence more often. You speak too much information.

PLAN OF ACTION: Actions to do after the session (goals): Realistic, Attainable, Measurable, and Specific

- Soldier will write essays on why it is so important to stay quiet in Formation and why discipline is an every day path for soldiering.

Individual Counseled: I agree I disagree with the information above.   DATE: 01 NOV 07

Soldier Name, Grade and Signature   John R Burnett Jr. E1   [signature]

Individual Counseled Remarks:

DATE: Name, Grade, Signature of Counselor

CIRCUMSTANCES AND SUMMARY (Include the expected standards and how the standards were not met)

PLAN OF ACTION: Actions to do after the session (goals): Realistic, Attainable, Measurable, and Specific

Individual Counseled: I agree I disagree with the information above.   DATE:

Soldier Name, Grade and Signature

Individual Counseled Remarks:

If such circumstances continue, you may receive disciplinary action under the UCMJ, or even be administratively separated from the Army. If a separation action is initiated to separate you from the Army, you may receive an uncharacterized discharge. An uncharacterized discharge may make you ineligible for veteran's benefits, and will prohibit you from reenlisting for a period of two years. You should however, consider this counseling to be an effort on my part to make you a better soldier. Stay focused and work hard.

IAW AR 635-200, this information may be used to document failure to attain required performance standards and may also be used to support non-judicial punishment or administrative discharge procedures.   SOLDIER INITIALS _____

Poor performance in these areas could result in punishment, New Start, or Separation IAW AR 635 - 200

Squad Peer Evaluations

To assist Soldiers understanding how they are viewed by their peers in the areas of; Teamwork, Motivation, Army Values and Contributions to the Squad. Consider Soldier actions and attitude when a Drill Sergeant is not present. Responses will be kept confidential. DO NOT RATE YOURSELF!

Name of Soldier: __Burnett__ Company: _A_ Platoon: _2_ Squad: _3_

1. Would you rate this Soldier in your squad as: ___ Top 3, ___ Average/Middle, _X_ Bottom 2-3

2. What are this Soldier's strengths, and does he/she have the potential to be awarded the Soldier or Soldier Leader of the Cycle? Explain: __The only one of his strengths - is that he is physically trained.__

3. In what areas does this Soldier need to improve? __He needs to Read and understand all Army Values.__

4. Does this Soldier live by the 7 Army Values? Is this Soldier motivated? Does this Soldier maintain discipline and military bearing? __He doesn't accept Army Values at all. He doesn't even know about what the meaning of the Army Values.__

5. Would you trust this Soldier to protect you and your fellow Warriors in combat? Do you think this Soldier would make a good leader and make sound decisions in Iraq or Afghanistan? Why or why not? __I would never trust the person, who thinks only about saving his own ass.__

Squad. Consider Soldier actions and attitude when a Drill Sergeant is not present. Responses will be kept confidential. DO NOT RATE YOURSELF!

Name of Soldier: Burnett Company: A Platoon: 3 Squad: 3

1. Would you rate this Soldier in your squad as: ___ Top 3, X Average/Middle, ___ Bottom 2-3

2. What are this Soldier's strengths, and does he/she have the potential to be awarded the Soldier or Soldier Leader of the Cycle? Explain:
He knows what hes doing but I cant thank he has the disciple to be soldier or the cycle of j

3. In what areas does this Soldier need to improve? discipline. Not talking in formation

4. Does this Soldier live by the 7 Army Values? Is this Soldier motivated? Does this Soldier maintain discipline and military bearing?
no He does not have discipline but he is motivated

5. Would you trust this Soldier to protect you and your fellow Warriors in combat? Do you think this Soldier would make a good leader and make sound decisions in Iraq or Afghanistan? Why or why not? I would tell him to combat with me but I would want him to be in a leadership position

To assist Soldiers understanding how they are viewed by their peers in the areas of; Teamwork, Motivation, Army Values and Contributions to the Squad. Consider Soldier actions and attitude when a Drill Sergeant is not present. Responses will be kept confidential. DO NOT RATE YOURSELF!

Name of Soldier: Burnett)   Company:____ Platoon:____ Squad: ✓

1. Would you rate this Soldier in your squad as; ___ Top 3, ✓ Average/Middle, ___ Bottom 2-3

2. What are this Soldier's strengths, and does he/she have the potential to be awarded the Soldier or Soldier Leader of the Cycle? Explain;

3. In what areas does this Soldier need to improve? He is immature. He tends to act like a child and he also talks in formation.

4. Does this Soldier live by the 7 Army Values? Is this Soldier motivated? Does this Soldier maintain discipline and military bearing? He does live by them. He is motivated, but he needs to maintain discipline. He could control his talking in formation.

5. Would you trust this Soldier to protect you and your fellow Warriors in combat? Do you think this Soldier would make a good leader and make sound decisions in Iraq or Afghanistan? Why or why not? I would go to combat with him. He would eventually maybe, it he could had some more discipline and stopped acting like a child.

Squad Peer Evaluations

To assist Soldiers understanding how they are viewed by their peers in the areas of; Teamwork, Motivation, Army Values and Contributions to the Squad. Consider Soldier actions and attitude when a Drill Sergeant is not present. Responses will be kept confidential. DO NOT RATE YOURSELF!

Name of Soldier: Burnett _____ Company: A Platoon: 2 Squad: 3

1. Would you rate this Soldier in your squad as: ✓Top 3, ___ Average/Middle, ___ Bottom 2-3

2. What are this Soldier's strengths, and does he/she have the potential to be awarded the Soldier or Soldier Leader of the Cycle? Explain;
Pretty good at PT and hes an expert marksmen.

3. In what areas does this Soldier need to improve? He tends to good DAT sometimes

4. Does this Soldier live by the 7 Army Values? Is this Soldier motivated? Does this Soldier maintain discipline and military bearing?
Yes he does and he is very motivated and disciplined. Hes squared away.

5. Would you trust this Soldier to protect you and your fellow Warriors in combat? Do you think this Soldier would make a good leader and make sound decisions in Iraq or Afghanistan? Why or why not? Yes I would hes a team player and doesnt get people hurt to shoot.

THE GOOD CONDUCT MEDAL

TO

SPC BURNETT, JOHN R. JR

ALPHA, 3RD BATTALION, 45RD AIR DEFENSE ARTILLERY

FOR EXEMPLARY BEHAVIOR, EFFICIENCY AND FIDELITY

IN ACTIVE FEDERAL MILITARY SERVICE

FROM   27 AUGUST 2007   TO   26 AUGUST 2010

THE ARMY ACHIEVEMENT MEDAL

TO   SPECIALIST JOHN R. BURNETT JR.
ALPHA BATTERY, 3RD BATTALION, 43RD AIR DEFENSE ARTILLERY

FOR EXEMPLARY SERVICE AS A PATRIOT OPERATOR/MAINTAINER IN SUPPORT OF OPERATION ENDURING FREEDOM. SPECIALIST BURNETT'S OUTSTANDING LEADERSHIP AND DEDICATION TO DUTY DURING OPERATIONS IN KUWAIT CONTRIBUTED TO THE OVERWHELMING SUCCESS OF HIS UNIT AND AIR DEFENSE OPERATIONS SUPPORTING THE U.S. CENTRAL COMMAND MISSION. SPECIALIST BURNETT'S PERFORMANCE OF DUTY IS IN KEEPING WITH THE FINEST TRADITIONS OF MILITARY SERVICE AND REFLECTS GREAT CREDIT UPON HIMSELF, THE 3RD BATTALION, 43RD AIR DEFENSE ARTILLERY REGIMENT, THE 69th AIR DEFENSE ARTILLERY BRIGADE, AND THE UNITED STATES ARMY.

FROM: 22 FEBRUARY 2010 TO 22 FEBRUARY 2011

THE ARMY ACHIEVEMENT MEDAL

TO

SPECIALIST JOHN R. BURNETT

ALPHA BATTERY, 3RD BATTALION, 43RD AIR DEFENSE ARTILLERY

FOR EXEMPLARY ACHIEVEMENT BY ATTAINING "FIRST PLACE LAUNCHER HOT CREW" DURING THE BATTALION BEST CREW COMPETITION FROM 26 AUGUST 2010 THROUGH 03 SEPTEMBER 2010. SPECIALIST BURNETT'S EFFORTS HAVE CONTRIBUTED GREATLY TO THE OPERATIONAL READINESS OF ALPHA BATTERY. HIS PROFESSIONALISM AND EXPERTISE IN LAUNCHER CREW DRILLS AND MAINTENANCE PROVED EXTREMELY VALUABLE. HIS PERFORMANCE REFLECTS GREAT CREDIT UPON HIMSELF, ALPHA BATTERY, THE 3RD BATTALION, 43RD AIR DEFENSE ARTILLERY REGIMENT, THE 69TH AIR DEFENSE ARTILLERY BRIGADE AND THE UNITED STATES ARMY.

FROM: 26th AUGUST 2010 TO 3RD SEPTEMBER 2010

THE ARMY ACHIEVEMENT MEDAL

TO

PRIVATE FIRST CLASS JOHN BURNETT
ALPHA BATTERY, 3RD BATTALION, 43RD AIR DEFENSE ARTILLERY

FOR MERITORIOUS ACHIEVEMENT DURING ALPHA BATTERY'S TABLE VIII CERTIFICATION. HIS EXEMPLARY LEADERSHIP AND PERSONAL COMMITMENT CONTRIBUTED GREATLY TO THE SUCCESS OF THE MISSION. PFC BURNETT'S PERFORMANCE IS IN KEEPING WITH THE HIGHEST TRADITION OF MILITARY SERVICE AND REFLECTS GREAT CREDIT UPON HIMSELF, THE 3RD BATTALION, 43RD AIR DEFENSE ARTILLERY REGIMENT, THE 11TH AIR DEFENSE ARTILLERY BRIGADE, AND THE UNITED STATES ARMY.

FROM: 26 FEBRUARY 2009 TO 11 MARCH 2009

THE ARMY ACHIEVEMENT MEDAL

TO

SPECIALIST JOHN R. BURNETT

ALPHA BATTERY, 3RD BATTALION, 43RD AIR DEFENSE ARTILLERY

FOR

EXEMPLARY SERVICE DURING THE A/3-43 ADA MISSION REHERSAL EXCERCISE. SPC BURNETT'S LEADERSHIP AND PERSONAL COMMITMENT TO EXCELLENCE CONTRIBUTED GREATLY TO THE SUCCESS OF THE MISSION. SPC BURNETT'S PERFORMANCE IS IN KEEPING WITH THE HIGHEST TRADITION OF MILITARY SERVICE AND REFLECTS GREAT CREDIT UPON HIMSELF, THE 3RD BATTALION, 43RD AIR DEFENSE ARTILLERY REGIMENT, THE 11TH AIR DEFENSE ARTILLERY BRIGADE, AND THE UNITED STATES ARMY.

FROM: 05 JANUARY 2010 TO 13 JANUARY 2010

♥ Appendix ♥

Dedication page- "My son, don't forget my teaching Keep my commands in your heart. They will help you live for many years. They will bring you success. Don't let love and truth ever leave you. Tie them around your neck. Write them on the tablet of your heart." -Proverbs 3: 1-3. The Holy Bible. NIRV, 1995, 1996, 1998.

Preface- "But the Farther will send the Friend in my name to help you. The Friend is the Holy Spirit. He will teach you all things. He will remind you of everything I have said to you."- John 14:26. The Holy Bible. NIRV.

Hello Friends- "Then does it not guide them when they see how many generations We have destroyed before them as they walk among their dwellings? Indeed, there are signs in that for those of intelligence."- Qur'an 20:128. Myislam.org. WEB.

Childhood Nightmares- "Even though I walk through the darkest valley, I will not be afraid. You are with me. Your shepherd's rod and staff comfort me." Psalms 23:4. The Holy Bible. NIRV, 1995, 1996, 1998

Confused Kid- "Faith is being sure of what we hope for. It is being certain of what we do not see." Hebrews 11:1 The Holy Bible. NIRV. 1995, 1996, 1998.

Troubled Teen- "So be careful. When you think you are standing firm, you might fall. You are tempted in the same way all other human beings are. God is faith-ful. He will not let you be tempted more than you can take. But when you are tempted, God will give you a way out so that you can stand up under it."- 1 Corinthians 10: 12-13. The Holy Bible. NIRV. 1995. 1996, and 1998.

No Parental Control- "And come not near to the orphan's property, except to improve it, until he or she attains the age of full strength; and give full measure and full weight with justice. We burden not any person, but that which he can bear. And whenever you give your word I.e., judge between men or give evidence, etc. SAY the TRUTH even if a near relative is at concern. And fulfill the covenant of Allah, this he commands you, that you may remember."- Quran 6:152. WEB. Quaranicquotes.com or al-quran.info 152

Uncle Sam's Nephew- "Brothers and sisters, God has shown you, his mercy. So, I am asking you to offer up your bodies to him while you are still alive. Your bodies are a holy sacrifice that is pleasing to God. When you offer your bodies to God you are worshipping him. Don't live any longer the way this world lives. Let your way of thinking be completely changed. Then you will be able to test what God wants for you. And you will agree what he wants is right. His plan is good and pleasing and perfect."- Romans 12:1-2. The Holy Bible. NIRV 1995, 1996, and 1998.

Sandbox Dramas "Hear all unwelcomed truths, study the writings of others, and write down your own thoughts."- Marcus Aurelius. 2021. Web. Insta@ marcus.aurelius.stoic

Answered Prayers- "Life is a circle of happiness, sadness, hard times, and good times. If you are having hard times have faith good times are on the way." - Buddha. Web. @ Parade.com

Why Me- "We did not wrong them, rather they wronged themselves. The gods they invoked beside Allah were of no help at all when the command of your Lord came, and only contributed to their ruin. Such is the seizing of your Lord that when He does seize the towns immersed in wrongdoing, His seizing is painful, terrible."- Quran 11: 101-102. 2022. Myislam.org. Web.

Autumn of Life- "So here is what I tell you. Every sin and every evil word spoken against God will be forgiven. But speaking evil things against the Holy Spirit will not be forgiven. Anyone who speaks a word against the Son of Man will be forgiven. But anyone who speaks against the Holy Spirit will not be forgiven. A person like that won't be forgiven either now or in days to come."- Matthew 12: 31-32. NIRV. The Holy Bible. 1995, 1996

Acknowledgments
&

A Special Thank You!

♥ First, I want to thank God and the Holy Spirit for every moment I get!

♥ Second, I want to thank my Granny who has help me in so many ways.

♥ Third I want to thank Grayson for showing me the light again.

♥Finally, I want to thank my parents, family, friends and everyone who helped raise me, for the life lessons and the love.

♥ Then to all the people I have met and crossed paths with. I pray, God is always in your heart, the Son shining on your path, and the Holy Spirit by your side. In Jesus name I pray Amen!

♥ Front and back, Cover pictures and designs- John R. Burnett Jr. Front cover picture is taken in front of childhood home East Lake Tohopekaliga, Narcoossee FL. Back cover Edgewater, Florida.

♥ Pictures throughout- Various family members & Friends.

♥ Printed & distributed by: bookbaby.com

Story Inspired & given the courage- By God, the Holy Spirit, and the son who sacrificed himself for our sins!